THE
JAM
1982

Copyright © 2022 Omnibus Press
(A division of the Wise Music Group,
14–15 Berners Street, London, W1T 3LJ)

Design by Lora Findlay

ISBN 978-1-9131-7269-5

Signed edition 978-1-9131-7291-6

A catalogue record for this book is available from the British Library.

Printed in Czech Republic.

www.omnibuspress.com

THE
JAM
1982

**RICK BUCKLER
& ZOË HOWE**

Dedicated to
the memory
of Simon Wells.

CONTENTS

*June 1977: The Jam (left
to right: Paul Weller, Rick Buckler
and Bruce Foxton) in action.
(Ian Dickson/Redferns)*

FOREWORD

BY GARY CROWLEY

How lucky was I that the first live gig I went to was The Jam?

The ripple effects of that fateful night at Battersea Town Hall on Monday 27 June 1977 were simply enormous for the 15-year-old me. As game-changers go, this was the equivalent of a Cristiano Ronaldo brace in the dying minutes of a cup final.

Me and my schoolmates were already caught up in the excitement and maelstrom of punk, and The Jam had quickly become my favourite new band. But witnessing the fire and skill Paul, Bruce and Rick displayed that night up close (I was at the front of stage, dead centre and could literally see the whites of their eyes) left me utterly reeling. I simply couldn't take my eyes off them.

Paul and Bruce jumped around the stage like synchronised trampolinists plugged into the National Grid whilst Rick sat steady at the back, pounding the skins on that jet-black kit, cool as fuck in those Roger McGuinn shades, keeping the solid beat which underpinned their revolutionary sound and led the charge of their musical attack.

The frenzied energy of their performance is something that I will never forget.

The shockwaves of my experience that night reverberated with me for months.

I vividly remember stumbling out of the town hall, jumping on the bus, talking ten to the dozen with my mates and still being soaked with sweat when I arrived at the other side of London in Lisson Grove. We were still reliving and dissecting what we'd witnessed that night in Battersea two weeks later.

Somehow, we knew that we wanted to be part of it… whatever 'it' was, and we quickly decided to hijack our school magazine – and turn it into a fanzine…

But that's a story for another day.

Looking back, The Jam really were an anomaly of their time. They had the edge, bite and vitality of punk but also an inbuilt pop sensibility that they'd imbued into their very being through their heroes, the greats of the sixties, soul and Motown. This was a pedigree you could really hitch your wagon to, there was a real sense that they could be around for as long as they wanted to be and, importantly, they were only a couple of years older than us. When you watched them up there on that stage, you could imagine, without any great stretch, it was you and your mates. The dreams of children.

It was all about the sound, the clothes, the live experience, the lyrics… they possessed a fire that few others could keep burning and, with each record, they got better and better.

Over six action-packed years, against a tumultuous political and cultural backdrop, this band held up a mirror to society and articulated the feelings of the youth so acutely, things would never be the same again.

Rick behind the kit in 1977. (Ian Dickson/ Redferns)

The band/fan relationship was the stuff of legend. Soundchecks became private gigs to younger members of their audience (some only in their early teens) who had missed out on getting tickets.

I've got some wonderful memories of chatting to fans from different parts of the country at some of those mini-shows and talking about our shared love for the band and our favourite new records. It was a real community.

The Jam released (amazingly) six albums across their relatively short career. Those records reflect a musical legacy almost as impressive as perhaps their main inspiration, The Beatles, while their run of singles, from 'In the City' all the way through to 'Beat Surrender', certainly puts them up there with the greats.

Always open to the new sounds and styles echoing around them, their music could be biting and explosive, packed to bursting with hooks and twists as on 'Absolute Beginners', then lurching to something as tender as 'English Rose' before hitting you with the perfection of 'Ghosts'… and then, in 1982, it was all over. At the very height of their popularity, there would be one last single and one last tour.

Rick Buckler was one of the three in the eye of that storm (four, if you count manager John Weller, which you absolutely should) and this book is his story, his account of that time, the band and their legion of fans.

And what a story it is.

As I said that night I introduced them on stage at the Golders Green Hippodrome in December of '81… 'Ladies and gentlemen… please give a magic hand for a magic band – Paul, Bruce and Rick – THE JAM!'

GARY CROWLEY, LONDON, 2022

*Playing the legendary Roxy
in Covent Garden, 1977.
(Erica Echenberg/Redferns)*

INTRODUCTION

BY RICK BUCKLER

From the moment I teamed up with Paul at school to start a band, everything else became secondary.

We started out as a three-piece, with Steve Brookes on lead guitar and lead vocals, Paul on his prized Hofner violin bass[1] and backing vocals, and myself on drums. We also had a name, which was needed; a name to go under at the clubs – not a very good name we thought, but it would do for now, until we thought of a better one: 'The Jam'.

Dave Waller, another school friend, soon joined on rhythm guitar, learning to play on the way. Rehearsing in Paul's bedroom whenever we could, we put together a set of covers from sixties hits: The Kinks, Chuck Berry and similar. We hurriedly put together an hour of music (quantity was needed, even if we couldn't play the songs well) as we worked towards our first gigs in Sheerwater Youth Club, at county fairs, and anywhere around the Woking area we could secure a booking. Paul's father, John Weller, being a taxi driver, knew all the clubs in the area that had bands playing at the weekends, and he was keen to help out with driving, borrowing vans and talking to the venues about 'his boys', as he referred to us.

Dave soon dropped out, being either fed up with the ribbing he received about his playing or the commitment required to show up when needed. His guitar, left at Paul's house, had the varnish scraped off the neck by Paul, which upset Dave – I think this was the last straw for him. In the meantime, we continued to go out as a three-piece, improving our set and adding in some rather dodgy self-penned love songs along the way. Bruce Foxton we had known from school was approached about the opportunity to join as rhythm guitarist, but he turned us down as he didn't like the sort of music we were playing.

Along with our choice of music to help secure bookings, we decided to adopt a uniform look. Looking back, our first try at this was embarrassing, with white satin bomber jackets, black shirts, white kipper ties and white teddy-boy shoes. We certainly were remembered by those who saw us. We had some press shots done which John would use to help with the bookings; I'm not sure whether we were booked because we looked professional or downright funny, but either way it worked for a while, at least until the outfits started to look a little shabby.

Gaining a good reputation at the local clubs for being reliable – with only a few complaints about the volume – we were soon busy every Friday and Saturday night somewhere in Surrey. John would come with us to all these shows, much to the annoyance of his wife. Not all venues took to us: the Midas Club in Woking thought we were too loud for their somewhat posh members, the Woking Conservative Club frowned

---

[1] *A nod to Weller's musical hero, Paul McCartney.*

upon Steve dancing on their grand piano during 'Johnny B. Goode', and he was chased from one side to the other in an attempt to stop him scratching the polished surface. This booking was short and singular.

A regular monthly slot at Woking's premier late-night hotspot, Michael's Club, for fifteen pounds a night helped with paying for petrol, and we could rehearse there on a Sunday afternoon. The shows were coming in thick and fast. Bruce had been approached again, and now, because we had plenty of work (and the band he was in did not), he decided to join on rhythm guitar. But we were not a four-piece for very long – Steve lost his temper one night when loading some equipment into a venue; he'd bashed his thumb and that was it for him, and so he left to start a solo career.

The money was never very good at these clubs, but we loved playing. So it was very disappointing to find that John was pocketing some of our fee for himself without telling us. If he had asked, I think we would have agreed for him to have it anyway, but the fact that he tried to hide this from us was not good and broke our trust with him. This led to myself and Bruce leaving Paul on his own. John tried to team Paul up with some older and more established acts from the clubs, but this failed on every occasion. Our own efforts to start a new band did not go well either, so when John begged us to come back with Paul, we agreed, picking up where we left off.

Seeing Michael's Club, this 'glamorous' dive, in daylight made us wonder why anyone would want to go there in the first place, but since it only opened after the pubs were closing at about ten o'clock, and most of the clientele were already well oiled by the time they went through the doors, the shabby wallpaper and general decor was so dimly lit, it didn't matter. At street level, a single door with a small square shuttered peephole at head height greeted those who desired entrance to this sought-after watering hole. Once through the door, a narrow flight of stairs led up to the bouncer, waiting at the top, to deter those who were not properly dressed. The bouncer was usually Joe Awome, whose talents were engaged with us again in 1979 as a 'personal' along with two others, Chris Adoja and Mono (deaf in one ear).

The ladies were always welcomed at Michael's Club, but as for the men, if you did not have a tie you could not come in. Joe Awome conveniently had a binbag full of ties at his feet that were available for a small fee. Some of the punters were known to be troublemakers and were barred. On one occasion, refusal led to the punter returning with his shotgun and blowing a hole in the front door.

We had a small curtained-off space behind the shoebox of a stage where we could get changed before the show; this space led onto a fire escape at the back. Below Michael's was a pole-dancing and disco establishment and, between sets, we soon found that if we were quiet enough we could descend the metal staircase and watch the pole-dancers getting changed. We were soon spotted, and a hurried retreat was necessary back up the stairs.

We wanted to be a four-piece like The Beatles, so efforts continued to look for a replacement for Steve. The 'band' ethic was important to us, as we saw the benefit in groups that we aspired to, the valued contributions each member made to the overall sound and image that went to create a stronger identity that solo artists often lack. For us, finding ourselves constantly being pulled into a three-piece made us play harder; musically, there are fewer places to hide as a trio. So we started to turn it to our advantage, exploring ways to make three sound like four.

In our early shows we organised ourselves and learnt our stagecraft; we wanted our own look and we developed our own sound. Despite our searches, all contenders for the fourth member failed. As a three-piece, we grew up musically with each other – until there was no room for anyone else. We continued to grow closer in forging our identity as a band in the years that followed. Our belief in and dedication to the band came before all other concerns.

The decision to leave the safe local clubs and try our hand in London was not welcomed by John Weller, but he did secure us a foothold in what was then the mid-seventies 'pub rock scene'. The social clubs around Surrey had become a ball and chain for us, and we were glad to leave them behind. They did not attract people because we were playing there, we were

Previous spread: The Top Rank, Reading on 13 June 1977. (Steve Morley/Redferns/ Getty Images)

Right: Rick: We often had impromptu press sessions at a venue and usually a photo was needed. This was taken in a store room behind the stage. Not very glamorous, but very 'street'. (Alamy)

just the turn for the night. We hoped to gain our own fanbase. London was a chance worth taking and our confidence and frustration drove us on. Three angry young men sweating, thrashing, loud in our defiance crashed onto the stage; it felt like we were taking London by the scruff of the neck, demanding to be heard.

The record companies could not fail to notice that these pub venues were full every night, buzzing with all the acts that were attracting their own fans. The punk bands also arrived with their own scene on the doorsteps of the all-powerful labels, EMI, CBS and even Polydor. In some ways there seemed to be a feeding frenzy from the record companies, not wanting to miss out on signing up these acts. Rumours buzzed amongst the bands about who would be signed first. What A&R people had been seen at their shows? The anticipation rose to add to the excitement. To be signed to a major company was the next goal for us. We had tried in the past to send demos into Decca. They responded:

Paul Wellae [sic] Esq.

Dear Mr Wellae,

We are herewith returning your demonstration tape. It has been listened to by our selection committee and found unsuitable for recording. We thank you for thinking of us.

Yours faithfully,
THE DECCA RECORD COMPANY LTD.

Other tapes that we sent in did not get a reply and the whole exercise proved frustratingly futile, fuelling our reasons to move into the London pub rock scene. 'The Jam' were certainly noticed by people our own age who filled the music pubs of London, and we were confident that, sooner or later, we would be signed. We knew that we were being watched, so to be asked to record some demos for Polydor Records brought us a step closer in the hope that the money men upstairs would give their approval.

I remember my dad calling me to say that John Weller was on the phone with the news that, after our demos had been reviewed, Polydor wanted to meet us at their offices with a proposal: a £6,000 advance for one single, with first option on an album if all went well. After reading about the much larger sums offered to other bands, £6,000 appeared very paltry, but a record deal was a record deal, despite it being with an unfashionable company. We thought CBS or EMI were much more sexy. The plain red Polydor logo at the centre of the vinyl did not thrill us either.

But Polydor did step up to the mark, and they had plans for us in the marketing of the records. Having our own logo stamped into the centre and bringing back picture bags all went a long way to help set us up as we headed towards our first release. We carried on playing in the London venues, but now we had something to shout about.

The 'In the City' single (1977) was well received by the critics, but more importantly for all concerned, it sold well, triggering the option for an album. Studio time was booked, and after eleven days in Polydor's in-house studio, we had a completed first album.[2] From here on, our feet hardly touched the ground: a long UK tour was now in front of us, along with plans to go to Europe and more single releases on the horizon. 'All Around the World' was released on 23 July, and by October, we'd had a short but intense trip to America with two shows a night in four towns over nine days. 'The Modern World' single was released on 5 November, with our second album *This is the Modern World* out the previous day, and more UK dates right up to 18 December. This was a flavour of what was to come.

We had something to prove, not only to ourselves but to the record company, and we intended to take it all on, make our mark and secure our place as a band. We carried this work ethic

---

[2]In the City *(1977)*

Rick in Tokyo,
July 1980.
(Koh Hasebe/
Shinko Music/
Getty Images)

Looking
serious in San
Francisco, 1977.
(Chris Walter/
WireImage)

Pinkpop Festival,
Landgraaf in
the Netherlands,
1980.
(Gie Knaeps/
Getty Images)

with us for the next five years. We knew how hard it was to stay in the music industry, so we did everything that was asked of us from Polydor, and more. *This is the Modern World* took the critics by surprise – it was not the same as *In the City* and the sales figures fell short of Polydor's expectations. Many thought that we had been signed too early. We shrugged these comments off, as our fanbase was still growing and the gigs were still buzzing with enthusiasm.

Our attention turned to our next album and Paul had hurried some demos to Chris Parry, our A&R man. His response? 'You are going to have to do better than this.' It was pointed out to us that, if a band had not established themselves by the third album, they never will. The real pressure was on. This next album would obviously take more than just songs, so we pulled out all the stops, we worked more on our own parts and all the arrangements, cutting out anything that was thought to be unnecessary and pooling all of our musical ideas as a three-piece. Our confidence in the studio environment had grown and we soon reworked the ideas into tracks that we were more happy with.

Vic Coppersmith-Heaven[3], with his experience and calm approach, was mostly responsible for our sound on record, and he was always a steadying hand if we ran into difficulties. We tried to lay all our tracks down as close to 'live' as we could, to retain that energy from our live performances, but we increasingly found that re-laying the guitar and bass tracks was becoming the norm for us.

The touring continued to be relentless, so soundchecks at gigs became the best time for us to routine new ideas. The extra work we put in in the studio paid off, as our third album *All Mod Cons* was critically well received, much to the delight of Polydor, and its release certainly proved to be a turning point for the band on the world stage. This meant more work in new territories, more releases and more demands from the record company. Our career was snowballing almost out of control but we had a fantastic agent and the hardworking promoters, along with Polydor's coordination, kept us very busy – which was just what we wanted. Planning was now well ahead by about six months and our lives were no longer our own. Recording commitments and releases as dictated by our record contract, along with tour dates and travel arrangements, were laid out well into the future. A professional tour manager was by now in place, Dickie Bell, and he was very much needed in our close entourage to coordinate between all other agencies. The money invested in us from all quarters demanded an experienced hand, especially on the road.

For the most part, everybody involved had a role in our working diary that left us to concentrate on being a band. The chain of decision-making came from Polydor, on whom we relied for our income, and fed down through recording and touring. We followed this schedule with more albums and singles and all the demands that came with them. The Jam was now a well-oiled machine and we loved it; not for one moment did we consider the cumulative effect this was having on our personal lives.

Renegotiating our record deals with more and more fiscal incentives blinded John Weller, with little regard to the pressure these demands were putting on us as a touring band and the demand for Paul to come up with more songs either for singles or albums. Releasing covers like 'David Watts' helped take the strain off. We were running down a well-trodden path that was becoming steeper and steeper, and, without proper consideration, something had to give. Within the band we continued to focus on what mattered most to us: the quality of the following albums, always taking a different approach to a new album, not becoming stale, and I think we achieved this. We are proud of the fact that we did not rest on our laurels. *Setting Sons*, *Sound Affects* and *The Gift* – in fact all of our albums – are distinct from each other and there is no reason why this wouldn't have continued to be the case, as we still had plenty of new ideas to explore given the time.

Single releases are an important showcase event for the record companies, and meant high-profile appearances on TV and radio. This was more the case then than now, with the likes of

[3]*Producer and sound engineer.*

Overleaf: Park West in Chicago, May 1982. (Paul Natkin/ WireImage)

the BBC chart dominating Radio 1, published every week in the big-selling music papers of the day: *NME*, *Sounds* and *Melody Maker*. A number one entry into the charts was the holy grail. We had growing sales in the UK on each new release and it was expected that we would soon attain what it took to reach the top slot: excess of 100,000 sales in a single week. Even so, it did take us by surprise when 'Going Underground'[4] went straight to number one in its first week of release. Still in America touring, we had anticipated that it would chart somewhere in the Top 10 and hopefully go higher in the second week on our return home.

The American tours were tough for us, especially Texas. Paul was not a big fan of America and had found it hard touring the United States as we tried to break into that lucrative market. Bryan Morrison, our publisher and the man behind such acts as Pink Floyd, T.Rex and later, George Michael, was with us at a show at the Starwood in Santa Monica in 1978. He'd come across a crowd of journalists patiently waiting backstage, wanting an interview with Paul after the show. They were from the likes of *The New York Times*, *Rolling Stone* magazine and *The Los Angeles Times* along with various radio and TV stations. Knowing the importance of the press in such a vast country, Bryan tried to get Paul to speak to them but he refused, saying to their faces, 'I've got more important fucking things to do than interviews with you lot.' We were lucky to have Bryan Morrison involved with us, but he was deeply disappointed that The Jam had 'possibly thrown away the best opportunity they were ever going to have, kissing goodbye to the USA forever'.[5] I think from that moment onwards it was always going to be difficult for us to get through to an American audience.

The overall view from us on hearing the good news from the UK was that we should 'get out of Dodge' and return to London as soon as possible to make an appearance on *Top of the Pops*. Our decision to fly back to England was welcomed by Polydor, so Concorde was immediately booked (why not?), cutting our US dates short. Although finally getting to 'number one' was fantastic for us, it was not a primary goal in our thinking. It also raises expectations on future releases: what if we fail to achieve this again? Are we to be considered to be going downhill? We felt that, in some ways, too much stock was put on this accolade and the sales figures that went along with it, but at that moment we could enjoy the glory and our position in chart history. It also meant that the demand for us to visit other territories was soon to increase, along with more 'product' (as the industry would say).

What could possibly go wrong now, after all the difficult hurdles were behind us and all the commitments and sacrifices made? We had established ourselves as a force to be reckoned with. It has to be appreciated that perceiving The Jam from a fan's point of view as opposed to our own experiences, being totally wrapped up in our own work, can at times seem very different. Becoming professional in 1977 we left behind a world of hopes and dreams and entered a more serious world of obligations to the contracts that we had signed, to give up some freedoms and totally commit to securing the success we had longed for. We continued to work hard and that crazy drive to excel was still with us, although in 1981 it could be said that there may have been little else for us to aim for. So many other acts had made that jump to the world of arena status, but this was a scary leap for Paul with the added pressure of being a frontman.

It could have been time to take stock, but without guidance in our business affairs, we carried on in the same way, buoyed up by our fans and our love of playing live. Then came 1982.

RICK BUCKLER, 2022

---

[4] *Released 10 March 1980 as a double A-side with 'Dreams of Children', 'Going Underground' was not included on any of The Jam's studio albums.*

[5] *Bryan Morrison,* Have a Cigar!*, Quiller Publishing, 2019.*

WINTER 1981

Severe snow storms batter Britain and temperatures drop to the lowest since 1874 | Arthur Scargill becomes the leader of the National Union of Mineworkers | The first case of AIDS is diagnosed in the UK | An opinion poll shows Margaret Thatcher to be the most unpopular British prime minister since WWII.

12–13 DECEMBER The Jam play the Michael Sobell Sports Centre, North London | **14–15 DECEMBER** The Jam, supported by The Ruts, Bananarama and Reaction, play the Hammersmith Palais | **19 DECEMBER** The Jam record a session at the BBC Television Theatre, Golders Green Hippodrome | Recording for The Jam's final studio album *The Gift*, which commenced in October '81, continues at AIR studios, London.

*The Michael Sobell Sports Centre
in London, December 1981.
(Steve Rapport/Getty Images)*

Richard Skinner, BBC Radio 1, 27 February 1982: The three of you swept the board in the 1981 NME *poll in every category.*

Bruce Foxton: *We were surprised. In 1981 we didn't really do a lot. We thought someone else was bound to sweep the board. In a way it's a bit disappointing.*

Richard Skinner: *Really?*

Bruce Foxton: *Well, that the general public don't recognise that there's someone else out there.*

Paul Weller: *There isn't anyone else out there.*

MAKING *THE GIFT*

RICK BUCKLER As I cast my mind back to 1982 to all the events that led to The Jam's demise, I found it was easy to forget everything else that drove the year on, too easy to funnel all the attention onto the impending end, and too easy to forget the anticipation I had for the upcoming shows, and the new releases.

We started recording *The Gift* – which would be The Jam's final studio album – just before Christmas in 1981. We always experimented when it came to recording: with *The Gift*, we'd taken a completely different view and had stripped everything back. We liked to try different studios as well, so we went to AIR[1], a fabulous studio on Oxford Street.

We never wanted to just do another version of the previous album simply because it sold a lot of records. Each album is markedly different from the last. I think we were constantly exploring how to be a three-piece.

PETER WILSON *producer* I wanted to record at AIR; they'd done a lot of recording at Townhouse Studios in west London and I think we all wanted a change. I knew AIR from my time there as tape operator in 1973. In that time I got to work on sessions with producers like George Martin, Chris Thomas, Tony Visconti, and great engineers like Bill Price and Geoff Emerick, and bands like Mott The Hoople, as well as Dave Gilmour of Pink Floyd. It was (and still is) a top-end studio, and then was well situated in Oxford Street[2] – very handy for Soho!

RICK BUCKLER We always recorded in London. Paul lived there, and it took a lot of pressure off;

Polydor knew that it would help if we didn't go off to Oxfordshire, or to one of Branson's big mansion studios and spend three months there: it'd drive us up the wall, it just wasn't our thing. We were much happier in London and being able to go home if we wanted to.

PENNIE SMITH *photographer* From 1979, I was heavy-duty touring with The Clash but I kept dropping in to The Jam, who were very well-organised, unlike a lot of bands that I worked with. Some of them were quite shambolic and would probably walk into a studio with unrehearsed stuff that just worked its way through when they started recording, but The Jam seemed a lot more workmanlike. Paul was quite bolshy, but The Jam were quite polite really.

RICK BUCKLER We were prepared, and we were good at putting songs together and just cutting to the chase and recording them. If we agonised over anything for too long, it went in the bin, because it wasn't happening. Me and Bruce would do a lot of work getting the arrangement right, because when it came to the recording, we would pretty much record it as live as we possibly could to keep that energy level up without over-producing it, without adding too many overdubs and redoing the bass and so on. Bang, put it down, and Paul was happy because he didn't have to sit there going, 'can't you guys get it right?'. [laughs] Basically, we had a formula and it worked for us. We knew what we were doing.

DENNIS MUNDAY *(A&R & product manager)*[3] The Jam were self-sufficient and they were professional to the point where I used to give them the schedule for the release of the singles and the albums – in those days it took twelve weeks to get

---

[1]*Associate Independent Recordings, founded by Sir George Martin in 1965. AIR studios, on the fourth floor of 214 Oxford Street, London, opened in 1970.*

[2]*AIR Studios has been situated in Hampstead since 1991.*

[3]*Interview conducted by Matteo Sedazzari, 2022.*

a record out, record it, get the sleeve designed, get label copy, and it's all at different times. So I'd say to them, 'Right, you want your single out on this date, deliver the label copy on this date, the tape on this date, and the artwork on this date.' And they went away and did it. In that respect they were one of the most professional bands I've ever worked with. Their records never came out late, and I never had any problems. There was the odd party and the odd broken door, but they weren't into smashing hotels, we just used to have a good drink. They were easy to work with, they didn't throw histrionics, they did it professionally. The schedule was heavy.

PETER WILSON It was pretty full-on although we didn't do silly hours, like some people who'd do all-nighters; it doesn't work when you are too tired to make sensible judgements.

RICK BUCKLER We used to have our offices in Nomis Studios; it was owned by Simon Napier Bell – Nomis is Simon spelt backwards. They had offices for bands, and storage and rehearsal studios. It was near Olympia, Sinclair Road. We used to see other bands come and go with their crews dropping equipment off and picking it up and going on tour and stuff like that. And I remember there were bands that didn't turn up for meetings or rehearsals, but the crew would turn up, set the gear up, and then sit around waiting for so and so to turn up. Two, three days, the drummer wouldn't turn up or somebody decided not to be in the country. And I remember thinking, 'we would never do that'. So there were bands that were less conscientious than we were; they were living more of the rock star life than we were. We were maybe a bit too working class for all that [laughs]. I don't know whether we suffered from it or whether it was a benefit, but it was the way we did things. Someone might oversleep and need to be woken up, but that was about as bad as it got.

DENNIS MUNDAY Pete Wilson had worked with The Jam on a lot of their demos, so in a way it was an obvious choice, it was a shoe-in. He knew the sound.

RICK BUCKLER We had worked with Pete Wilson before, when he was Polydor's in-house engineer. We found that he was a great help to Chris Parry[4] on the *In the City* album, when Chris had taken on the role of producer. Always wanting a different approach – and

in a new environment – Pete helped us achieve an individual sound for *The Gift*.

PETER WILSON Prior to recording *The Gift* I had recorded two singles with The Jam – 'Absolute Beginners' and 'Funeral Pyre' – so I hadn't spent much time with the band. I'd got a job as a recording engineer at Polydor Studios in 1975 when I left university. It was at their head office, then in Stratford Place just off Oxford Street. There I worked with a variety of people – Alexis Korner, Bill Bruford, Brian Eno. In 1976 and 1977 punk was kicking off and major record companies like Polydor were chasing to sign emerging bands: there was the idea that punk could be the next big thing so record companies wanted to get in early. Polydor chased The Sex Pistols and The Clash amongst

Paul poses for a portrait on the roof of AIR studios in Oxford Circus during the recording sessions for The Gift, January 1982. (Erica Echenberg/ Redferns)

---

[4]*Parry co-produced* In the City *with Vic Coppersmith-Heaven.*

others and netted Siouxsie and the Banshees, Sham 69, The Cure and The Jam in 1977. Chris Parry the A&R man was instrumental in much of this, and he went on to co-produce the earlier Jam recordings.

DENNIS MUNDAY I was their product manager and their A&R manager. The A&R manager takes care of the music side – if they need session musicians, book the studio etc. And I would say as the product manager, 'right, The Jam have got an album coming out in November,' and it's my job to make sure it does come out in November.

PETER WILSON Polydor Studios saw a succession of bands coming in to record demos for the A&R department, bands like Chelsea and Shane MacGowan's The Nips. That's how I came to work with The Jam after they signed to Polydor. They would come in to rehearse songs and try out things. Paul would often book a day or two to come in with his guitar tech, Dave Liddle, and demo new songs. If we had spare time we would record covers for fun, some classic soul tunes like 'Stand by Me' and Beatles songs like 'Rain', 'And Your Bird Can Sing' – fun for me as I got to play drums on 'Rain' and organ on 'And Your Bird Can Sing'. Of course, this was at a time when Paul was digging the later Beatles music; 'Start!' obviously reflects that, and so does the backward tape fragment on the start of 'Dreams of Children' (*Sound Affects*).

PAOLO HEWITT *music journalist* You could always tell where Paul was at with their covers – it was at *Sound Affects* time he was covering The Beatles' 'And Your Bird Can Sing' and stuff like that. And there was an Eddie Floyd song they used to do too – he can't help himself, he had to do covers.

PETER WILSON I think every band starts as a covers band – almost every song on The Rolling Stones' first album was a cover, and similarly with The Beatles. That's how you learn your trade. But recording these covers was as much about Paul's affection and respect for these classics – he is one of the most ardent music fans I know.

PAOLO HEWITT Then he reads *Absolute Beginners*, and realises that the mod that he knew down in Woking – The Who, 'My Generation', '66, '67 thing – actually started in London much earlier, and centred around jazz. *Absolute Beginners* is

about this kid going to jazz clubs and the multiracial thing, that hip language... all that stuff was a huge influence on him. Then he saw all the connections: Ronnie Scott's, John Coltrane, the Flamingo, the mod clubs – these are the roots of it all.

STEVE NICHOL *trumpet, Loose Ends* I was connected to The Jam through the saxophonist Keith Thomas; he introduced me at the last minute because the person that was supposed to be doing the gig, Frank Burke (Frankie B), couldn't make the dates. I went down to Nomis for an audition and ended up recording that day. Paul liked what he heard so it just escalated from there. I was 21, straight out of Guildhall School of Music and Drama.

It was fun – they were treating us like one of the boys, basically. We'd sit down and play cards with them, especially Paul – and he always won! [laughs]. Rick was always playing around with his camera. He was taking loads of pictures, and Twink was around as well at the time, taking pics.

NEIL 'TWINK' TINNING *photographer* I got involved about December 1981. I used to work for Kodak; I'd been a friend of Rick's for a number of years, and I got the job of processing all the band's films, holiday snaps from Weller, and so on.

RICK BUCKLER Inviting Twink to document us behind the scenes was of real benefit. Most of the photographs of the band were very much of the same old predictable formula, live shots or us lined up somewhere, not smiling and generally posing. So to have Twink with us all day recording the more candid movements of life on the road was very refreshing, and gave him unequalled access that nearly all other photographers could not have. He also had a very much-needed talent as a photographer: to see 'the moment' and act on it.

NEIL 'TWINK' TINNING There was a lot of recording going on at the time, so I'd go into the studios and take a couple of snaps and hang out with rock'n'roll people. It was fabulous.

EDDIE PILLER *founder / MD Acid Jazz Records, Jam fan* The Jam were the main focus of what we called the Mod Revival, which, by 1982, had changed substantially and seen most of its adherents getting into soul, jazz and R&B for the first time. We were changing in terms of the ideas and clothes and everything else that we were into, and I think that the

Paul at the Michael Sobell Sports Centre. (Steve Rapport/ Getty Images)

'When people are singing football chants and ruining the support act's performance by chanting for The Jam the whole way through, then you wonder if you're getting through.'

PAUL WELLER TO MARK COOPER,
RECORD MIRROR, 17 JULY 1982

fashion had changed completely from what we wore in 1979 to what we wore in 1982. It was almost like a different scene. As The Jam changed, a lot of their fans changed with them.

STEVE NICHOL Paul wanted more of a Motown type of sound, so he wanted the trumpet and the saxophone. I think the transition into R&B did not sit too well with some of the fans, as a large number was from the skinhead community. The Michael Sobell gig[5] scared the life out of me, let alone Bananarama, who were the support for that gig. A huge skinhead presence.

GARY CROWLEY *broadcaster, Jam fan* I've got memories of the Michael Sobell Sports Centre that December. The Bananas were on before The Jam, and I remember Sara Dallin and Keren Woodward saying that there were a few coins lobbed their way.

NEIL 'TWINK' TINNING Rick had said, 'come up and do the Michael Sobell Centre'. That's where I took the long shot in the corridor. They were just sitting backstage having a fag and discussing what they were going to do for their second encore. While we were backstage, all you could hear was, 'WE WANT THE JAM. WE WANT THE JAM.' It was going crazy.

RICK BUCKLER We'd played the Rainbow Theatre so many times, and we wanted to find an alternative venue in London, so the Michael Sobell Leisure Centre in Islington fitted the bill. In the past there'd been trouble outside the Rainbow between skinheads, mods and punks, and the feeling was that we were hoping to leave those days behind us by this point, but

sadly this was not the case. We were lucky never to be directly involved.

PAUL WELLER *to Paul Lester,* **Uncut**[6] There were always fights at gigs. You were guaranteed it was going to kick off at the end of the gig. Even walking around London was a violent thing at the time. At gigs, beer mugs would come at you – that's if people liked you.[8]

EDDIE PILLER It was nothing out of the ordinary, if you were going to see The Jam, to be attacked by skinheads. It was a very difficult time.

GARY CROWLEY It was quite violent back in the early eighties. You had to be a fast runner if you came out of the gig and you walked into the wrong sort of crowd. You had to be pretty lively.

JAMIE TELFORD *keyboards, live band / 'Beat Surrender'* Paul used to put his pet bands on the support sometimes. Weirdly enough, about a year before I joined The Jam on tour, I was in a band called Everest The Hard Way, and we supported The Jam because we had the same agent. We played in Stafford, and I remember it was the biggest stage we'd ever known. We went on there and just froze.

GARY CROWLEY A lot of support bands would get short shrift from The Jam audience because some of them were quite blinkered in a way, and I think Paul found that very frustrating. I can't talk for him, obviously, but I think he found it frustrating that they weren't open to different things, or to coming at it from a different perspective.

STEVE NICHOL At least the mod fans thought the move into more soulful music was really cool – they were already into Motown and appreciated that style of music.

PAOLO HEWITT There was definitely a mod thing about that. When these 14-, 15-year-old Jam fans were putting The Who and The Jam on the back of their parkas, we were like, 'that's really not mod, mate. Listen to R&B.' The other thing that was happening was that *The Face* magazine took over from the *NME* as the go-to publication. In the seventies, the *NME* was where it was at. I grew up with it and I was obsessed with it, we all were, obsessed with the writers... when I moved

---

[5] *12 December 1981.*

[6] *Paul Lester, 'Paul Weller: Last Man Standing', Uncut, December 1998.*

to London and I could buy the *NME* on the Tuesday lunchtime at Camden tube it was like, this is Nirvana! I'd have to wait until Thursday afternoon in Woking.

But with *The Face*, what happened was that clubs started taking over from rock venues. There was this swinging London thing and these clubs were turning up – Le Beat Route was one, St Moritz... and it was black music. Black music was really making an impact in London, and there was a kind of turning away from rock music, in a way.

GARY CROWLEY You've got to think back to that time; in 1981, rock became almost like a swear word. We had Haircut 100 saying in interviews, 'we're not doing gigs, we do happenings.' I think Paul felt more in tune with that line of thinking. It wasn't about going to gigs any more, it was more about going to clubs. Dance music was, to use an old sixties expression, where it was at, if you look at *The Face*, the singles of 1981 and 1982, and there was a lot of amazing black music being made. We're beginning to hear amazing records coming over from America from Grandmaster Flash, Afrika Bambaataa, and white boys were taking their cue from a lot of those records they would have grown up listening to pre-punk as well. So, whether it was ABC or Haircut 100 or Spandau Ballet, The Jam – especially Paul – were taking inspiration from a lot of those records.

PAOLO HEWITT Paul's musical taste at that time was Northern soul, rare soul, funk, and that's why we have songs such as 'Precious' on *The Gift*, and later 'The Bitterest Pill', 'Beat Surrender' and they did the Curtis Mayfield cover ['Move On Up']. So Paul was moving away from The Beatles and more towards black music. Paul was always looking for things to inspire him and I think that London club thing was inspiring to him.

GARY CROWLEY There's a guy called Ad Croasdale – he was the DJ on the Trans Global Unity Express tour in 1982 – and Paul credits him for turning him on to a lot of black music, early Curtis and stuff like that. I think Paul's always had a passion for soul music, but Ad was an important influence.

PETER WILSON 'Trans-Global Express' clearly references US funk, as does 'Precious'. 'Planners Dream' uses a steel pan ensemble, which is an unusual choice and gives a very different flavour to the music. 'Town Called Malice' has strong echoes of sixties Motown, more explicitly than other tracks they had done.

RICK BUCKLER[7] I used a drum pattern that is very familiar to most people. It has that Motown-type feel that makes people want to dance. I used a tambourine too, which kind of enhances that snare; I heard that Ray Davies is particularly fond of that snare sound.

DENNIS MUNDAY It was something I always thought had to happen the move into funk and soul. They were growing all the time and they were changing. If you listen from album to album to album, I think that was a greater change than any of the other changes.

MAT OSMAN *Suede bassist, Jam fan* I think another reason they loved soul music, there's that hardcore, hardworking professionalism; James Brown fining his band for every bum note, there's something of that relentless 'we've got one chance at this, let's get it right.' They were so tight as a three-piece, they were absolutely incredible. Rick is a brilliant drummer, and you don't get that good by mistake. Bruce and Rick meshed together perfectly.

PETER WILSON Something I loved about The Jam's music was the vocal harmony between Paul and Bruce; really powerful and effective, adding a great dimension to the music without being sweet – often quite the opposite when the song or lyric demanded it. So even as a three-piece band they could deliver so much playing live. Adding horns and keys was an understandable development, and showed the direction Paul would take with Style Council, but as a three-piece band they were great.

'PRECIOUS', 'MALICE', '5 O'CLOCK HERO'

STEVE NICHOL Between Keith Thomas and myself, we worked out arrangements for certain songs. 'Precious' was quite funky and came about in quite an off-the-cuff way. Paul had been thinking for some time about being a bit more soulful. I think he felt very comfortable introducing that feel into the situation.

PETER WILSON 'Precious' started as a demo; I made a literal tape loop of a single bass drum beat and recorded five minutes of that onto a track of a 24-track tape. This is pretty much before drum machines and

---

[7]*Rick Buckler, Ian Snowball, The Dead Straight Guide to The Jam, Red Planet, 2017.*

Rick: Paul loved recreating poses of one of his idols – Steve Marriott – when being photographed. (Twink)

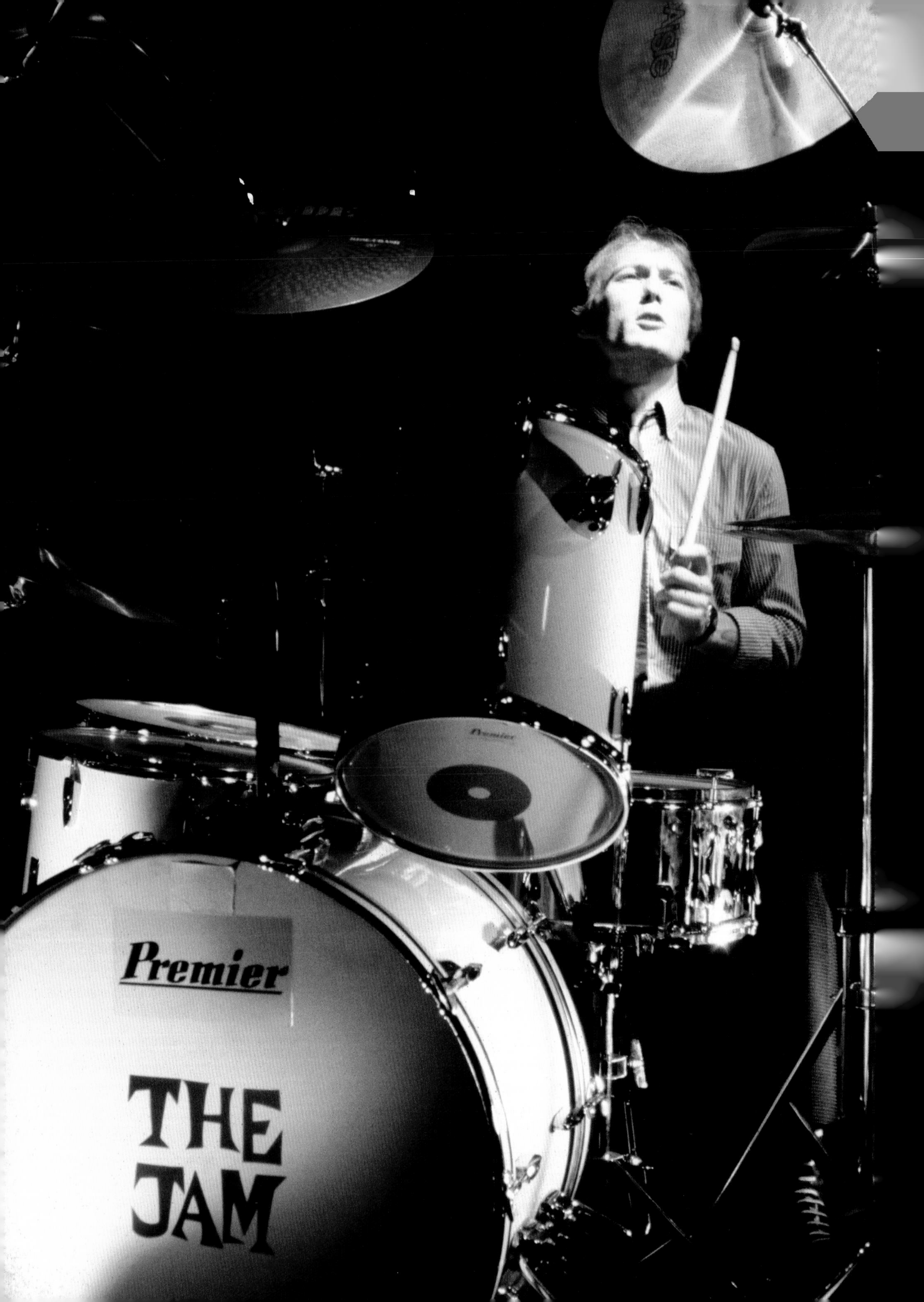
Premier
THE JAM
Premier

NEW YEAR 1982

Unemployment figures exceed 3 million for the first time since the 1930s | Sales of tabloid newspapers are on the rise | During a concert on JANUARY 20, Ozzy Osbourne bites the head off a bat that has been thrown at him, assuming it to have been fake.

The Jam complete work on *The Gift* and prepare to promote and tour the album | Double A-side 'Town Called Malice' / 'Precious' is released on 29 JANUARY, debuting at number one in the UK singles chart | 18 FEBRUARY The Jam perform both songs on *Top of the Pops* | 24 FEBRUARY marks the first live show of the year for The Jam at London's Central Polytechnic, with The Alarm and poets Attila The Stockbroker and Little Brother in support.

Chris Salewicz to Paul Weller, The Face, 1982: You speak out against the notion of heroes. Yet you yourself certainly are one.
Paul Weller: Yeah. And that pisses me off. Because it's a trap... ultimately it will trap me and the group as well. That's my one big worry – that we'll become institutionalised, and that'll be that. If we split up there are other things I could do, but it wouldn't be the same at all. It's a long time now: it's eight years we've been together – a long fuckin' time. But we understand each other's temperaments.

RICK BUCKLER At the beginning of the year we were happy to be back on the road again and the diary was being filled well in advance, pre-tour and studio rehearsals, getting ready for future recordings... after all, things were still going very well for the band, and demand for product from Polydor, singles etc. and gigs, was high. John was boasting that Paul was now a millionaire, a remark that turned my and Bruce's heads as we were still watching our personal spending. We had the understanding from John that any money coming to The Jam account was to support future touring expenses. It was becoming more and more apparent that something was wrong with the band's financial situation.

We had started the year with all the usual enthusiasm. A new album just finished, and the anticipation of taking it on the road, starting with a tour in the UK, (always a very satisfying endeavour to launch off with), dates in America and Japan already pencilled in and plans for more releases. We still had a real love for playing live, especially with the great reception we were receiving at every single show and the dedication from our fans.

We did not see it at the time, but the stress of this workload was beginning to show, especially in our private lives. The gap was widening from our old way of life and the rock'n'roll bubble was now closing in around us. Throwing ourselves into each and every tour left little room for anything else, but as the year started we were loving it, and Polydor were only too pleased to keep the work coming as the demand grew with our popularity.

Christmas somehow seemed to me more like being told to 'tidy your room first' before playing with one's toys: I do like the festive season, and we certainly needed the time back in the real world. But *The Gift* album was unfinished and for my part I was keen to get the year underway.

NEIL 'TWINK' TINNING In January 1982, Paul asked me to shoot the album cover for *The Gift*. They were doing a song called 'Running on the Spot' at the time, and I got the impression from Paul that he felt like he was running on the spot, he couldn't get any further forward. That was the concept behind the cover. We did the photographs on the top of AIR Studios.

BRUCE FOXTON[1] Right on the very top of the building. Very precarious up there.

RICK BUCKLER One at a time we ran on the spot while Twink shot away...

NEIL 'TWINK' TINNING If you look at the contact strip of Paul Weller and flick through the photos, he doesn't look very good when he's running on the spot! Bruce looked fantastic, but Paul was all over the place.

RICK BUCKLER To take a moment during studio time to organise a photo shoot for the front cover of the album was tricky. So we decided to go up on the roof of AIR Studios. One at a time we ran on the spot while Twink shot away. I remember that just as we thought that we had it in the bag, Bruce saw that Paul wore trousers in his shots and not jeans so he wanted to reshoot his photos and dashed off to change into trousers as well. I don't think anyone noticed the difference. Originally the photos were to be in black and white on the front cover, but I think that a more colourful look was suggested by Polydor so the tint was added.

NEIL 'TWINK' TINNING As usual, Bruce wasn't happy with the shot – he wanted to change his trousers – so I had to do him again. It didn't make any difference: the shot that went out was the first one anyway.

A couple of months later, I remember walking down the high street in Aldershot and seeing all *The*

---

[1] *Gary Crowley interview with Bruce Foxton and Rick Buckler for DVD release* From The Jam – A First Class Return, *Invisible Hands Music, 2008.*

*Going down
a storm at the
Central London
Poly, February
1982.
(Steve Rapport/
Getty Images)*

*Paul at
the Central
London Poly.
(Steve Rapport/
Getty Images)*

'Not since The Specials' 'Ghost Town' has a record so well captured an urban mood and sent out its own warning: "Better stop dreaming of the quiet life / 'Cause it's the one we'll never know / And quit running for that runaway bus / 'Cause those rosy days are few."'

PENNY VALENTINE, 'LETTER FROM BRITAIN: JAMMED UP, JELLY TIGHT', *CREEM*, JUNE 1982

Gift merchandise in Woolworths. When they did an album, they would have big cardboard cutouts in the stores. When I saw it for the first time I thought, 'this is what it's about'. If I look back, I would say that's the highest I've ever been mentally, walking down the street and seeing that stuff.

THE RELEASE OF 'MALICE'

RICK BUCKLER After an album was finished, final mixes and running order all in place, we would often have a review, inviting record company and publisher to attend for their thoughts. Choosing a single was usually a forgone conclusion but there was not a doubt here for 'Town Called Malice'

DENNIS MUNDAY 'Malice', that was straight out of the box. I mean, that was going to fly. It was always going to be 'Malice' and 'Precious'.

PAUL WELLER[2] 'Town Called Malice'[3] has become something of an anthem and a folk song at the same time.

RICK BUCKLER I love 'Malice', our third number one single and a double A-side with 'Precious'. It is to this day, I think, our most popular single, judging by

the amount of plays it gets.

The promotional video for 'Town Called Malice' was shot in AIR Studios. There were several rooms in the studios, so we just cleared some space in one of the larger rooms and used that. The video had a simplicity to it that we liked. Like 'That's Entertainment', it was quite dark. The crew only used a few spotlights, which they pointed in the direction of Paul, Bruce and myself, and for the video we also included Keith Thomas and Steve Nichol. In the video Paul chose to not hold his guitar. Instead he grabbed the microphone and sung into that. The finger-clicking worked well, as did the slogans that someone wrote onto pieces of card. One said 'Anti Complaney League Baby!'; whoever wrote it misspelled what should have said 'complacency'. The second one said, 'If we ain't getting through to you, you obviously ain't listening.'

We never really took to making promotional videos. They were always put together in a hurried fashion without much in the way of planning. The days that were set aside to shoot them were squeezed in around other commitments, like recording albums or singles when we were known to be in town and not out on tour. Along with the hanging around, waiting for the film crew to set up, and the restrictive budget, the time allowed to get any results was only one day.

TOP OF THE POPS

RICK BUCKLER[4] Videos were fast becoming more important with the emergence of MTV in America, but in the UK, the shows were too few to take full advantage of the medium, apart from *TOTP*, who frowned on the use of video and preferred that the artist appeared in the BBC studio (albeit miming), or the more serious music show *The Old Grey Whistle Test*. The latter went out late at night and was more likely to accommodate a video. But the BBC were slow to move with the times and a half-hour show to present the nation's Top 30 was long thought to be too short.

There is this sort of fight that goes on for bands, that you have to be so much better than everybody else, and that pressure is put on you from all sides, whether it's the *Top of the Pops* thing and who's gone before and who you're supposed to live up to, or the

---

[2] *Paul Weller promotional interview for the release of* The Gift 30th Anniversary Deluxe Edition, *UMC.*

[3] *The song title is a play on the title of the Nevil Shute novel,* A Town Like Alice.

[4] *Rick Buckler, Ian Snowball,* The Dead Straight Guide to The Jam, *Red Planet, 2017.*

venues and the logistics of it all. Just to get yourself off the ground was difficult in those days; I think that sorted the men from the boys in a lot of ways.

As 'Town Called Malice' was a double A-side with 'Precious', the BBC asked us to perform both sides on *Top of the Pops*.

STEVE NICHOL To do a doubleheader on *Top of the Pops*, that was quite stressful. But it was a cool thing as well, so you had mixed emotions. There was some pressure there – the only other band that had done that before was The Beatles.[5]

We were supposed to just do one song, and that was 'Town Called Malice', but then, because it was a double A-side, the bosses at *TOTP* said, 'Oh, we'd like you to do this as well.' It was kind of strange, because it only happened on the day.

DENNIS MUNDAY It was a tremendous achievement. To play both songs, it's amazing. I know they were well chuffed. But the thing with *TOTP* is that it's very boring.

STEVE NICHOL The *TOTP* experience is totally artificial. You're performing to a backing track, you're just miming to your song, really. And then there's only a handful of people. It looks like there's more than that. There's no more than forty people in the crowd, and the actual studio is quite claustrophobic. Then at the back you can see other people wandering around, you know, other stars and hangers-on from the record companies that wanted to come as well.

DENNIS MUNDAY You're there all day, you rehearse – camera rehearsal, dress rehearsal – it's a long day. I can't say I ever enjoyed it, and obviously you can't get pissed. After the show, we all just hit the green room.

RICK BUCKLER Still, being asked to perform both 'Precious' and 'Malice' on *Top of the Pops* – what an honour for us.

PETER WILSON 'Precious' and 'Malice' are both excellent but 'Malice' is definitely more 'radio friendly' – it still gets lots of plays on Radio 2. Like many of The Jam's songs,

despite the 'sweet' elements in there there's an edge in the lyrics and the vocal delivery that is really compelling.

RICK BUCKLER A lot of people assumed 'Malice' was about Woking – I think it was just as much about London. But this is why people relate to this stuff: it could be any town. Paul was good at observing what was going on, not just immediately around him, but in the towns we went to on tour.

MAT OSMAN At school, it was very tribal – you had punks, you had metal kids and the 2-Tone kids – but The Jam were everyone's band, especially coming from the Home Counties suburbs where you felt terminally uncool. It was always all about London, so to have someone like Weller who was young and had that scruffy Estuary accent and sang about suburban places was incredibly important. He sounded like people I knew.

RICK BUCKLER Paul left Woking as soon as he had the chance. Bruce and I stayed; we weren't ever at home anyway, we were always on the road. Also Woking is close to London, so if we were rehearsing or recording, or doing press, London's pretty much the hub, the record company is there, and the agent's office and all that stuff. So it wasn't like we had to move from, you know, Banff in Scotland to try and stay in touch. It was only down the road.

London was also incredibly expensive. Even in those days, we couldn't afford to have done it. In the early days, Paul just rented somewhere, but Paul's rent on his flat was more than my whole mortgage – and it wasn't a comfortable move. People soon found out where he lived, so he had bars on the windows and stuff like that. People used to follow him home late at night after the shows. All those things that I think he was trying to get away from in Woking just followed him, really. When he was living in Woking with his parents, flocks of scooter guys would turn up outside their house – which really annoyed the neighbours. But Paul primarily moved to London because he just liked London… I think he was in love with the idea of London.

But the important thing is that Paul found there was value in writing about the stuff that was going on around you. This is what we see going on around us. You know, the fights and the violence and the uncertainty of people losing their jobs. You can't keep writing love songs.

---

[5] *The double A-side 'Day Tripper' and 'We Can Work it Out' in December 1965.*

Rick: The split of The Jam is often misunderstood. We hadn't fallen out with each other and we generally got on well. After we parted it became clear that there was something about our business that troubled Paul.
(Twink)

SPRING 1982

3 MARCH The Queen opens new arts venue the Barbican Centre in the City of London | **6 MARCH** 'Town Called Malice' is toppled after three weeks at UK number one by Tight Fit and 'The Lion Sleeps Tonight' | **2 APRIL** marks the start of the Falklands War.

12 MARCH The Jam's sixth studio album *The Gift* is released | **12 MARCH–8 APRIL** Trans Global Unity Express tour (UK), preceded by a 'hometown' show at Guildford's Civic Centre. Supports on the Trans Global Unity Express tour include The Dolly Mixtures, Belfast punks Rudi, and The Questions | **16 APRIL–30 APRIL** The Jam take the Trans Global Unity Express tour to Europe.

Paul Weller to Mark Cooper, **Record Mirror, July 1982:** *All that stuff about me being a leader is crap — I'm as confused as the next person.* The Gift *isn't intended to be sanctimonious or self-righteous, I just wanted to make a record that would motivate people, that would move you emotionally and make you want to stand up and have a clearer vision of what things are really like. I'm not trying to get people to join the Communist Party but to make them feel alive.*

THE RELEASE OF *THE GIFT*

MARK BRZEZICKI *Big Country drummer, Jam fan*
We had The Jam on constant rotation and we were really excited about the next album coming out. I hooked on to The Jam along with Simon Townshend, Pete's younger brother – I was in his band and he got quite obsessed with The Jam. You know when you're young and you're in a band, you hang out around people's houses? We tended to gravitate to Simon's house, and we would open up the new Jam album and look at what gear they've got. For me it was like, 'what's that kit Rick's using? Single-headed toms? Is the Union Jack on there?' All those little details that you look for.

MAT OSMAN The music press cooled a little with regard to *The Gift*. It's almost like once they moved into much funkier stuff, you could feel some of their early fans stepping away from it. It also felt in the press like it was a step too far from what they saw as 'the roots'. I don't remember it getting as good reviews as *Sound Affects*.

KEITH CAMERON *in* **NME**[1] *The Gift*'s attempts at experimentation fail – albeit gloriously in the case of 'Trans-Global Express', abjectly with the steel-drum farrago 'The Planner's Dream Goes Wrong' – and its best moments are the desolately lovely 'Carnation' and 'Running on the Spot'. That their singles now routinely entered the charts at number one merely emphasised the fact that The Jam had become just another facet of the corporate pop machine.

SIMON WELLS *music writer, Jam fan*[2] *The Gift* was an uneasy mix of soul, gospel and punk-funk, sowing seeds that would only begin to fully germinate once Weller had moved on from the creative confines of The Jam.

EDDIE PILLER *The Gift* was my least favourite Jam album; I didn't particularly like it. My favourite was *This is the Modern World*, then *All Mod Cons*, then *In the City*. Then *The Gift*, and then... the other one [laughs].[5]

VALERIE SIEBERT *in* **The Quietus**[4] Their sixth and final record, *The Gift* is only barely a Jam album, so it's fairly unsurprising that many fans of the band wouldn't rank it among the group's best. It's Weller with one foot out the door, only a Jam album with a Jam sound because Bruce Foxton and Rick Buckler are making themselves known. A rhythm section so distinctive that their timbre comes through on even the most divisive of Weller's musical sidesteps.

MAT OSMAN People do like bands to stay the same – what you need is these tiny little changes. At the time, I would have happily had another *Sound Affects*, but you don't write albums like *Sound Affects* and *The Gift* without being ambitious and wanting to change all the time. I would have hated them to stay what they were on *All Mod Cons*. I liked it when the soul influence fitted into it. You can't have interesting, ambitious music with someone who wants to stay the same.

PAOLO HEWITT I knew when *The Gift* came out that the end was close. Oh God, yes. It's got 'Ghosts' on it, which is a very key track that shows where we're going musically, but the rest is a bit of a mish-mash. I think Paul wanted to do all this stuff but couldn't do it within that thing.

DENNIS MUNDAY *The Gift* was different – completely different. There were only really three or

---

[1] *Keith Cameron, 'Direction Reaction Creation', NME, May 1997.*

[2] *Simon Wells, 'The Jam: 11th December 1982', Modculture. co.uk, September 2011.*

[3] *Setting Sons, 1979..*

[4] *Valerie Siebert, The Quietus, 2012.*

'Despite the preceding clarion call of 'A Town Called Malice', by the time of The Gift you have to suspect Weller knew the game was up.'

KEITH CAMERON, *NME*, MAY 1997

Not sure what's taken Bruce's breath away… (FG/Bauer-Griffin/Getty Images)

four what I would call 'Jam tracks' on there. I mean, things like 'Precious', 'The Planner's Dream': they wouldn't fit on previous albums, while some of the other tracks, 'Carnation', 'Ghosts'… 'Malice' you could say was a typical Jam track.

MAT OSMAN You can see the seeds of the rest of Weller's career in 'Ghosts', deliberately uncomfortable being comfortable, the minute he feels pinned down, either by the press or by himself, he immediately takes on something else. You could feel that Weller wanted a different kind of band. It was interesting to watch Talking Heads go through

almost exactly the same thing. David Byrne didn't want it to sound punky, he wanted it to sound Latin and funky and he did a similar thing – he basically augmented the band. You started getting other people coming in, like Adrian Belew, backing singers… and it's almost like you can see him building the music that he wanted around him and the rest of the band being pushed to the back.

PAOLO HEWITT This is what I think: I think they'd had a year off before *The Gift*, or at least took time off. But the trouble with The Jam was, it was just England. They would go to Europe and America, Japan and all those places, but it wasn't really happening for them the way it was happening here.

It was becoming predictable. I mean, how many times were they going to play the Rainbow?

Previous spread: Time for tea.
(Twink)

The Palladium in New York, May
1982, on the Trans Global Unity
Express Tour. (Ebet Roberts/Redferns)

Band and crew take a break from the tour bus to admire the view at Snake Pass, Derbyshire. (Twink)

RICK BUCKLER When we first started to tour professionally around the UK, our mode of transport was a Ford Granada, with the three of us, John and a driver. Having a car was very useful but we soon got fed up with being squeezed in along with our luggage. A small minibus was tried for a while but long before 1982 we had found that a coach was best; we could get up and walk about and space was not a problem. There were some seats with tables and plenty of room for extra travelling guests, girlfriends or journalists, etc. We had maybe not the best touring coach that the industry had to offer but it had an extra area at the rear with a television, a reasonable stereo and very comfortable seating. The tables at the front were mostly used by John, Paul and Kenny (Paul's personal roadie) where the favourite pastime was cards, always gambling with large amounts of cash. As soon as the journey of the day was underway so were the bets. I sat in only once: failing to win anything, I soon bailed out. Gambling had never been my thing, and I could not afford to lose like that on a daily basis.

STEVE NICHOL I enjoyed the fun. I didn't like playing cards so much – I always used to lose. One time we were at Glasgow Airport and our flight was delayed, so we sat down and we were playing cards and one of us was up about 100 odd quid, then the next thing Paul Weller wins it back... It got a bit expensive. But we were getting good money, so it was all right. They looked after us.

RICK BUCKLER Twink was our official photographer and spent a lot of time on the road with us in that last year. Our bus pulled over at Snake Pass in the Derbyshire section of the Peak District, crossing the Pennines, and we got out and had an impromptu photo shoot sitting by the side of the road. Paul's Dansette Major also came off the bus with us and can be seen in some of the other photos from this session.

NEIL 'TWINK' TINNING We had to get from Leicester to Manchester over the Snake Pass, and the coach took us on this scenic route, so we stopped and did photographs. Quite a nice story: we stopped at a pub, so if you can imagine there's a Jam tour bus, all The Jam, minders, me, management, all sitting outside this pub, and all you could hear was The Jam album playing out of somebody's car. They came into the car park, blasting it out. Somebody outside of the circle, they've just come to this pub and he's got The Jam's album playing in his car – suddenly he sees the whole band's there! That was quite a spooky experience.

RICK BUCKLER It had been difficult for some time to stop at the regular service stations without being mobbed by fans, so we tried to find places off the beaten track for lunch. On most occasions there were only about ten of us on the bus, but country pubs and cafes would display a sign: 'No Coaches', in an attempt to stop their business being overwhelmed with too many people for lunch. Some establishments would try and shut their doors, lock up and turn the lights out when we pulled into the car park.

One day, after driving through several small villages searching for a suitable eatery, we just had to stop somewhere despite the signs – the need of a drink, or 'the call of nature' forcing the issue. On this occasion, being denied entry Kenny relieved himself on the front door that had just been slammed and locked on us. Shouts of 'I am calling the police' could be heard from inside. So we always made sure that there was plenty of booze on board, usually rescued from the dressing room or the hotel the night before. Each morning the sound of chinking bottles was to be heard as the coach was loaded up for the day. Having to be on the road promptly also meant that Paul was often seen being pushed onto the coach dressed only in his overcoat. None of us were particularly good in the mornings, but we did have all day to get ourselves together. Each show day, we only lived for that hour and a half on stage and we got through the rest of the day in whatever way occupied us best.

After the show, on returning to our hotel, a get-together in the bar had become a fixture to end the day: an indulgent habit that was international and suited us well.

NEIL 'TWINK' TINNING You'd stay in a place like Holiday Inn, and I used to room with Rick – two double beds, so I had great access. The Jam liked having their photo taken and they trusted that I wouldn't put out anything that was derogatory. When I did the first one of the Trans Global Express down in Portsmouth, I was doing the usual rock'n'roll photography stuff, you know, and it was, 'no, no, no. We don't want any of that. We want candid shots behind the scenes.'

PENNIE SMITH The Jam were tight visually and weren't as tactile as The Clash, but once they'd got used to me and started ignoring me, that was great. I love going invisible. The mod thing involved tight suits and standing straight, so when they stood in front of the camera they were a bit like clothes-hangers, like old-school school photos. Once they'd forgotten

Behind the scenes on the Trans Global Unity Express tour. (All photos Twink)

I was around, whether they were going on to a soaking-wet stage in Stockholm or eating sushi in Japan, they'd make more ordinary shapes. I've got a lot of informal Jam stuff.

NEIL 'TWINK' TINNING Rick was really interested in photography, as was Bob Jeffries, the monitor engineer, and we used to sit in the hotel and get blasted, talk about photography, depth of field and all that sort of stuff. We even hired a medium-format camera on Rick's American Express card.

RICK BUCKLER Photography was a great hobby for me on the road. I would have my Canon A1 and a small collection of lenses with me all the time. I never really badgered the professional photographers that we came across except Twink, about cameras and things. When touring in Japan, I would spend all my money on lenses within the first few days and never had much left over for anything else, and of course it was all on film which was expensive to process.

NEIL 'TWINK' TINNING I'm one of the founders of The Jam photographic club – not many people know about The Jam Camera Club. A lot of people on tour used to give me their films to develop; Bruce's always had to be delivered in a brown paper envelope, for obvious reasons. We used to get knocks on the hotel room door, and we had special knocks so we knew who was coming into the camera club. Some weird pictures came out of those nights. It was purely a social thing more than anything else.

RICK BUCKLER The hotels by that time were much better. They didn't shut the bar and there was always food available. We could unwind, locking out the world; this was 'our time'. All the demands of the touring schedule were temporarily suspended. Sandwiches and copious amount of drink were laid on. I could not drink at all before the show, so I had become the only sober one to leave the stage each night. I just could not function on alcohol unlike Paul, who started almost as soon as he got out of bed or, for Bruce, his festivities started around lunchtime with the familiar sound of a beer bottle top hissing.

At each venue the promoter would supply us with some snacks in the dressing room, about twenty-four bottles of beer and soft drinks, two bottles of vodka for Paul, two bottles of Bacardi for Bruce and two bottles of 'Bull's Blood', a full red wine for me. I saved mine until the day's business was done.

CHRIS SALEWICZ *in* **The Face**[8] We talk in Weller's room at the Leicester Holiday Inn. There is a Cromwellian, puritanical obsessiveness in the manner in which Paul Weller continually returns to railing against what he defines dismissively as 'those pop groups' – the likes of Depeche Mode and Adam Ant – betrayers, he believes, of the destiny of their musical form.

On the floor is an open copy of a history of the French Revolution. 'I just read anything that interests me,' he says. 'I don't think I've got such a thing as a favourite novelist, apart from Orwell.'

His own publishing company, Riot Stories, is shortly putting out a fanzine with its own flexidisc, as well as another volume from Newcastle poet Aidan Cant. 'I'm definitely going to expand the publishing thing,' he threatens. In addition, Weller and The Jam now run two record labels, Respond, distributed by Polydor, and Jamming, which they themselves put into the shops.

Occasionally he visits the cinema, though he seems to be invariably disappointed. Carry On films are his favourite: 'I saw an advertisement for *Death Wish II*: it seemed to have all the ingredients for a box office success – a few rapes, a few murders. To me it all just adds to the fuckin' sickness. The other week I saw *Heartbeat*, that film about Kerouac. But I wasn't impressed. I'm not impressed with The Beat Generation anyway. It's the same with Burroughs. I read one of his books when I was at school – *Junkie* – I thought it was a load of crap to be honest – another big myth.

'What about the music papers, though?' he suddenly demands. 'I think they're terrible!'

Anyway, I hear you've given up drinking...

RICK BUCKLER Paul would often throw up by the side of the stage before the show – nerves, maybe? I think there was a fear of sobering up and the inevitable hangover was not welcome during our set. A short period of Paul trying to lay off the drink was tried after his stomach blew up like a balloon – this did help his health but did not improve his mood. John thought it was best if he started drinking again as soon as he could.

[8]*Chris Salewicz, 'The Paul Weller Interview', The Face, May 1982.*

JAM-MANIA

GARY CROWLEY Without sort of pouring it on, they could probably lay claim to being 'the people's band' – it was either The Jam or The Clash. They had this unique special relationship which spilled over to the point where Jam soundchecks kind of became gigs in their own right. They would let a lot of the kids in who hadn't got tickets, let them in for the soundcheck and they'd watch fifteen, twenty minutes.

RICK BUCKLER We'd play two or three numbers, and they'd come in, get stuff signed, and go again, you know. Anybody that could get to the show at four o'clock in the afternoon, we'd always let them in. We got to know a lot of these people personally, and they would turn up at different shows during the same tour. On one occasion, they actually turned up at the studio late at night – I think I was the last person to leave, and they said, 'Oh, we've come to get Rick, we want to take him across the road to the pub.' It was that sort of relationship. We didn't think anything of it, but I don't know whether other people get that, where the fans literally turn up and say, 'right, we're taking you to the pub.' It's quite fabulous. And to be honest, I was absolutely knackered, and I remember thinking, 'I can't, not again...' But fans would come along and just chat to you like you're their old school friend or an old mate.

When we did the first shows in London, a few of the fans used to realise that if they got to the Red Cow or the Nashville or something like that in the afternoon, they could get in free, because there was nobody on the door and the bar staff were working, preparing for opening time. With most of the places, you'd load the gear in through the front door, they'd turn up and it was just a continuation of that sort of attitude – even at the Brighton Conference Centre. The venues were completely unprepared for having anybody coming in during the day.

EDDIE PILLER I was 18, 19 at the time. We just followed them everywhere as a matter of course, and utilised every opportunity we had. It was a major social event of our lives, going to see The Jam.

We started going to see The Jam in a coach: a friend of ours, Simone Lynch – a girl from Chigwell – her dad owned a coach and he would drive us all to see The Jam, places like Utrecht... in fact I can remember very well Rick getting on the coach one day and saying, 'Why are you guys here in this Dutch outpost?' Fifty 16-year-old kids from Woodford. I always appreciated Rick for doing that.

Paul, Bruce and
NME *journalist*
Danny Baker.
(Twink)

Rick: Keith Thomas tried to give
me some pointers on how to play
a trumpet. Although I may look
convincing in this shot, the noise
I made was not very musical. (Twink)

*Rick: We didn't like these moments
before going on stage, because we
were all ready and just had to wait.
Was Paul doing a last minute
adjustment to his underwear? (Twink)*

I saw The Jam probably fifty-three times. I probably only legally got in forty times. Occasionally I'd be on the guest list for Paul Weller or the support bands, but there was also the passing of guest passes... you'd go in, get a guest pass off somebody, and you might already have a backstage pass, which was a cloth sticker. You'd go in, you'd go up to one of your mates who had one, get his one, go outside, give his one to someone else, go back in and repeat the whole procedure. That way thirty people would get in with two passes. We did it at every gig.

RICK BUCKLER Fans used to get themselves in with the crew, and the crew used to play along with it. They'd walk through the front door, or they'd hide in the toilets when they were supposed to be locking everything up. In the end, they used to send people around looking in all the empty rooms, sweeping all the fans out. I mean, it used to annoy the hell out of the venues because these people hadn't paid, and I don't know how it affects things like insurance, if there'd been a fire and there were more people in there than there should have been. It all just went totally against the grain. But we just did it, it was just something that we continued to do from the very early days of playing the clubs in London to right the way through to the end.

We had 'bodyguards' – there were three of them, and they were taking turns with whom they worked: either myself, Bruce or Paul. Kenny Wheeler was usually with Paul; we used to call him 'the gooseberry' because he used to hang around with him and Gill all the time. Then there was Chris Adoja and a guy called Joe Awome, an ex-boxer: he'd actually fought Muhammad Ali in an exhibition fight. He was a lovely guy but disliked minding Bruce as he found him hard work. Joe Awome used to come to where I lived in Lightwater and pick me up in the mornings, and we'd go off to the recording studio, that sort of thing. Joe went back a long way with us; he used to be the bouncer of a club we used to play at in Woking called Michael's. I think that's how he got the job. They weren't just bodyguards, but it was more like somebody who could ferry us around, pick us up and drive us places, go and get the dry-cleaning and stuff like that; they had multiple roles.

But it was, I suppose, because we used to meet a lot of people. It did have its moments when, say, at the end of the show, we couldn't get out of venues because there were so many people waiting outside. We made a rod for our own back in some ways, because it was always, 'oh, we just want this signed, you know, just have a quick chat, come and have a coffee afterwards.'

'We haven't become an institution, people have started to treat us as one. It's accepted that we're a big band as if that's all we are. We don't need to be accepted, we need to be encouraged, pushed on, motivated!'

PAUL WELLER TO MARK COOPER,
RECORD MIRROR, 17 JULY 1982

PAUL WELLER *to Paul Lester,* Uncut[9] It was great at first, because we was popular – we'd started to take off. Then all of a sudden there was 100 people outside after the gig, and then there were 500. I kind of retracted from that point. Put up a wall a little bit. It was a bit freaky for me. We was trying to say, 'We're the same as you', but once something blows up big... it gets increasingly difficult.

RICK BUCKLER There was an occasion when we came out of a venue and Paul had an old college scarf on, somebody grabbed it from one end, and somebody grabbed it from the other and the poor guy's getting strangled. You know, there were occasions when somebody had to untangle him.

The coach would pull up out the front, and then we'd dive out the back, get into the promoter's car and disappear, otherwise you just wouldn't get out. We used to dash sometimes from exit to exit to see whether we could actually make it out, but the fans weren't silly: they used to be crowded by this door and crowded around the front and there was another crowd by another fire exit... so that was uncomfortable. Yeah, mania. There was a lot of that – and it just got more intense during 1982.

NEIL 'TWINK' TINNING At the end of the gigs they were so hot when they came offstage, literally dripping with sweat, and you're giving them a towel and whatever, and Paul used to take the mick out of me because he tried to get me to sell his sweaty underpants to the fans. Of course I was really naive and stupid, 'I'm not doing that!' Would have made a fortune.

[9] *Paul Lester, 'Paul Weller: Last Man Standing',* Uncut, *December 1998.*

George Orwellish. I remember Paul had been reading this book called *The Vision of Albion* about King Arthur, there was a kind of English mysticism that he loved.

MARK BRZEZICKI The Jam were tapping into the past, but making it very new and exciting.

RICK BUCKLER The Who had obviously been through all this before us. The early days of The Who, they were regarded as a sort of mod band, and we were almost retelling a similar story, you know, the *Meaty Beaty Big and Bouncy* album where all the songs are really short and precise, little stories – much like The Kinks did, and we were doing that as well.

I suppose we got to the point where you have to leave something behind, you have to move on from just playing ordinary large venues to transcending into what you'd call arena rock. We never actually did it, for obvious reasons. But I think that becomes quite difficult, because that disconnect between you and the fans just becomes absolute. I think there was a bit of that, that this was a little bit scary if we were going to go into that. We were starting to do the Wembleys and that sort of thing. There was always pressure for us to go and do the States – we'd been to the States and supported Blue Öyster Cult and Angel and Be-Bop Deluxe and all those bands that were playing 30,000-seaters, and we were at the bottom on the bill. So we knew what these big shows were like, when there's an audience standing there with cigarette lighters up – it looked absolutely stunning.

It's all right when you are at the bottom of the bill, even though nobody likes you when you go on stage, you know [laughs], 'Who are these twits? We're here to see Blue Öyster Cult. We've got three guys in suits. What?' So I think there was that sort of scenario. The Who had done it quite successfully. They'd made that leap – most bands do: Queen did it. The Beatles fell foul of it, because there just weren't the venues to do that sort of thing in those days. They did the Hollywood Bowl, but they didn't have the PA. Nobody could hear them! So the whole journey is fraught with difficulties.

Paul met with Pete Townshend – I think they spent an afternoon in a pub – and I don't think they got on quite as well as Paul had hoped, because Pete Townshend's quite matter-of-fact about the business, you know, 'this is what happens, this is the way you do it', and [The Who] had made that leap from playing larger venues to being mega, really, a proper

'Most of the people I met within the punk scene were all trendy wankers. Once it started filtering out to the suburbs, it got a whole lot more interesting. It was all going on out in the sticks. The whole 'boredom' thing meant more in the suburbs. They couldn't see that in London, with all the stuff that was fucking going on.'

PAUL WELLER TO PAUL LESTER, *UNCUT*, **DECEMBER 1998**

worldwide act. And I think the realisation of some of the things that Pete Townshend was telling Paul just didn't go down well at all. You have the music and the band and the songs, but when you actually have to deal on a sort of business and monetary level, that's completely different. And it shouldn't be the realm of the band, but how else do you keep control over what you're doing?

MARK ELLEN The Jam had such a devoted fanbase; we even did a special where we interviewed all three of them, which had only ever happened before with The Police – a major indication of status. I remember Rick talking about all his early jobs – in a fishmonger's and a drawing office and places that made motorcycle parts, rubber gaskets and medical equipment. Asked if he was worried that his livelihood depended on Paul writing songs, he said, 'well, if he stops writing then he'll be out of a job too,' which suggested he hadn't considered a world in which Paul carried on, but in another group, without him.

Previous spread: The Danish TV Show Spil Op. *(Jan Persson/ Redferns)*

Right: (Twink)

'I've always respected bands that have been able to call it a day. I think you owe it to all the people that have supported you not to become an embarrassment. I just think it would be horrible if The Jam were still around in 10 years' time. I still believe in that old-fashioned idea of not selling out — that statement from the punk archives.'

PAUL WELLER TO MARK COOPER,
RECORD MIRROR, 17 JULY 1982

The Palladium in New York on the Trans Global Unity Express Tour, May 1982. (Ebet Roberts/ Redferns)

SUMMER 1982

16 JUNE Welsh miners go on strike | **14 JUNE** Falklands War ends | The first child of the Prince and Princess of Wales – Prince William – is born on **21 JUNE** | The Provisional IRA detonates two bombs in central London on **20 JULY**, killing eight and wounding forty-seven | *Complete Madness* by Madness reigns in the UK album charts.

14 MAY–5 JUNE The Jam embark on their sixth US tour, followed by their third tour of Japan, **11–17 JUNE** | **26 JUNE** The Jam play at the Rangers Stadium, London, on their return from Japan | **3 JULY** Single 'Just Who is the 5 O'Clock Hero?', a Dutch import, is released | **AUGUST** Paul Weller tells Rick Buckler and Bruce Foxton that he wants to break up The Jam.

Richard Skinner, BBC Radio 1, February 1982: I've got a feeling that this LP might well be the one for America, especially that second track, 'Ghosts'. I think that is potentially an American hit record.
Paul Weller: American success to me I equate with compromise and watering down. I don't see it happening anyway, so I'm quite optimistic about that.

RICK BUCKLER It's difficult in England to get into the music industry; things always seemed to be against you, not least because we don't have proper venues and it was all a bit ad hoc. In the early days it was pubs, clubs and old cinemas, which are not really set up for music. In the States, it's a whole different ball game, the whole thing is set up for it.

The first time we toured America we played in small clubs, just what we were used to in the UK. As our popularity grew at home, so did the venues, the hotels and the transport improved, but when we toured other countries for the first time, we found that we had to almost start again on the lower rungs of the ladder. By 1982 the audiences were already familiar with us, no longer were we a support act to be 'checked out' or a club act working hard to get press attention. Going back to Europe, Japan and the United States was now becoming more like touring the UK. The record company was happy that their investment in tour support, all their planning and guidance was paying off, increased record sales and the intense amount of work that we had put in over previous years were now securing our position on the world stage.

NEIL 'TWINK' TINNING I'd become The Jam's official photographer after *The Gift* shoot, and Paul had wanted me to do the American tour, but the label wouldn't pay my flight or anything like that – I'd have to fund it myself and sleep in the tour bus...

Weller leant on Polydor to get me some cash from *The Gift*, and that was meant to fund my flight to America. But I was 21 and I just didn't have the savvy to know how to do that.

I've been doing a lot of 'what ifs'. Bryan Morrison took over The Jam's publishing around that time; I could have gone to him and said, 'Look, I've got this access, will you fund me to do this?' The record company wouldn't do it. I said to Paul, 'what about doing a book?' He didn't want to do a book. But he wanted me to do the American tour, and I didn't do it. I wish I had.

What if Paul hadn't upset the American press like he did? Bryan Morrison had set up a lot of good press, including *Rolling Stone* magazine. But apparently Paul wouldn't do the interviews. Just wouldn't do them.

RICK BUCKLER Bryan was nobody's fool but had a heart of gold and a very cool head, and his advice should have always been listened to. He knew what successful bands had to go through, and the privileges that came with the territory, having seen it all before. This wider view was yet to be appreciated by Paul.

BRYAN MORRISON Sticking to his punk-rock principles, he was wary of press and playing 'the media game'... Paul never quite came to terms with the fact that his rebellion against the system could go only so far; he also needed that system to spread his message.[1]

RICK BUCKLER Paul has this reputation of being grumpy, mostly because he takes too many things too seriously and he was never very good with relationships. There were times when you could see that Paul was about to burst when something was bothering him and he did not have the skills to deal with it, often taking it out on people around him. When he was in a good mood he was completely different, more like his old self.

BRYAN MORRISON They never had a hit in the States. It was a travesty.[2]

RICK BUCKLER I truly believe that Bryan Morrison was a real fan of The Jam, and music in general. He had been around the music industry for a long time and he understood that it was also about people.

NEIL 'TWINK' TINNING Bryan Morrison understood the power of the band, Paul's writing in particular. What if Paul had done those interviews? Would The Jam be as big as Pink Floyd? The press

---

[1] *Bryan Morrison,* Have a Cigar!, *Quiller Publishing, 2019, p.144.*

[2] *Ibid.*

Tickets and posters from North American and Japanese shows.

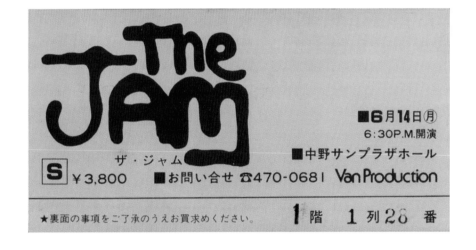

Rick: We were finally making headway in the States, and after a tour of north America, we looked forward to a very enthusiastic welcome in Japan before heading back to the UK and the storm to come. (Koh Hasebe/Shinko Music/ Getty Images)

Rick: Taking photos of a band on stage is hard enough with the changing light and movement. Twink did a great job in a difficult environment – he was very capable at spotting the moment. (Twink)

'Your future at least
looks mapped out, but
what about the other
two? Some people
are saying, aren't you
dumping them?'

'Well, that's a load of
crap, isn't it? We work
together as a group. It's
not my responsibility.'

PAUL WELLER INTERVIEW,
NATIONWIDE, BBC TV, 1982

So, despite sound reasoning from myself and Bruce, Paul could not be swayed from his course to leave the band.

Bands fall by the wayside for all sorts of reasons: death; falling out between members, management or record company; a lack of sales or success; or the euphemistic 'musical differences'. But none of these applied to us. There was obviously something else going on behind this decision. As a band we would have respected Paul's decision to leave, but the way in which he had intended to carry this out, and the reasons for doing so made no sense, nor did it give any credit to how we had arrived where we had.

Nearly all decisions about the band's work, and therefore our schedule, came from Polydor, and it is true that overall control and guidance was in their hands. One thing Paul did not like, and we felt the same, was that we were being told when to come up with singles and albums, along with the touring and promotion required to support sales around the world, all at the record company's behest. There was nobody with the foresight or strength to stand up and say to Polydor that the workload was too relentless, nor did we realise that finally we were now in a position to call a lot of the shots.

KEEP CALM AND CARRY ON

RICK BUCKLER Between the three of us, one of our strengths was to always step up to the mark, no matter what was demanded of us. From the very early days we had the ethic that we enjoyed and wanted to work as much as possible, but this came with a price on our personal lives and on our health that could not be sustained.

NEIL 'TWINK' TINNING I actually can't remember a time when they didn't put 100 per cent in. They were just committed and doing the gigs. I think Bruce had a big, big problem with the developments. Rick was fairly steady. But once I knew things were going not very well with the band, because of the split, there was a bit of 'them and us'. You know, there was a general parting of the ways.

RICK BUCKLER As far as the socialising between us three, that tended to get a bit fragmented; Paul spent a lot more time with Gill – you know, windswept walks and sitting on swings – whereas we used to socialise between ourselves, me and Bruce, and I used to hang out quite a lot with the crew. I mean, you just

get through it, you find a way of getting through those sorts of things.

PENNIE SMITH It's possible that I sensed the end perhaps because I was just being called in less, there was less intimacy going on and they didn't particularly want it to be known. At one point I was seeing them extremely regularly, 'we're doing this, we're doing that, a video going on, we're going to Japan, do you fancy coming out?' Then, slowly, I wasn't involved as much. I know there was another photographer, Twink, doing a lot of stuff with them, but of course I work in a peculiarly idiosyncratic way, I tend to inadvertently embed myself in bands to the extent that they can let me completely wander about as and when I want, so often, if things perhaps aren't going right, I'll find I haven't been invited. I don't know, I can't really explain it, but I distinctly remember seeing them less towards the end.

NEIL 'TWINK' TINNING When a split happens, you think you're still in the book, but you're not – you don't get access any more. Whereas previously I could wander anywhere I wanted, I had to be more of a reportage sort of photographer, like just, this is what I see, this is what goes on.

RICK BUCKLER Previously we'd always made a point, if we were going to do any press, 90 per cent of the time it was all three of us that did it. You know, if we turned up to do an interview with whoever it was, or a photo session, it would be the three of us. It was only really in the last six months when Paul decided that he was going to leave that we suddenly realised that Paul was doing a lot of press on his own.

Someone at the time said, 'Well, there's three guys in The Jam, and two of them are not called Paul Weller.' There was this terrible sort of 'me, me, me' thing beginning to happen. I don't know whether that was generated by the press, or somebody in Paul's ear saying, you know, 'you don't need these other two guys', but there was a certain amount of backlash from John after the band had split, where he started to call us 'hangers-on' and things like that. And I thought, 'well, that's not entirely fair.' I think both myself and Bruce sort of brushed that off, because I think John felt quite bad about the fact Style Council didn't really take off in the same way as they'd hoped, and I think that caused a lot of tension within their camp.

The reasons Weller would later give publicly for splitting the band up, I think they were just complete

'It's best to quit when you're on top. You can't go much further than The Jam. Splitting now means you can hold your head up high. I'd hate us to go on like The Who because people don't look at all the good things you've done. They just focus on the crap. To me, The Jam will always mean something and it will never lose that meaning.'

PAUL WELLER TO BARRY CAIN, *FLEXIPOP*, 1982

Left: (Twink)

twaddle. They looked good in the press, but it really didn't make a lot of sense in the scheme of things. It was a romantic idea, you know, 'I'm making the band into a legend by doing this.' I don't know. It's difficult to assess exactly where Paul's head was during that last year. Really, I mean he must have seen the audience and the way that everybody really loved the band.

In the past, especially from the time we were signed up by a major label, we had talked about the longevity of other bands and artists that had gone before, the vagaries of fame, money and the music industry in general, the effects that it has on those involved could so easily turn into vanity, greed and self-importance, and the knock-on effect this has. When we first started out in youth clubs, working men's clubs and our move into the London pub rock scene, we were so full of expectation and hope, it was so straightforward; back then, we were not tainted by ego or fame. For my part, I had emerged relatively unscathed.

I realised that 'nothing lasts forever', we had achieved a lot – maybe more than we had ever hoped – made some great friends and experienced so much. I still look back with very fond memories of being part of something that meant a great deal to so many others. The Jam had set us on a course that defined the rest of our lives. For the band to end in this way was like suicide or self-destruction, a permanent solution to a temporary problem of mismanagement.

The pretence that it was a grand gesture was obviously dreamt up in his own mind to ease his unrest with what he must have known by then to be a grand mistake. The real reason? Paul will never bring himself to reveal. I strongly suspect it was related to the way John had handled his title of manager, and would explain why Paul did not want to talk about The Jam or to myself and Bruce face to face after the split, and have to answer awkward questions.

Overall, it was the way in which it was done that annoyed us: 'The Jam' – our sound and our image – had come about with all of our input and dedication; Paul's attitude, that he had achieved it all by himself, was clearly self-centred. The internal repercussions and reasons of the break-up obviously impacted differently outside of the band but the fans were as equally distraught about the news; they were our fans and moreover we were theirs. Despite efforts to keep the break-up a secret for a long as possible, the cat was soon out of the bag. We didn't really have a lot of control over that.

The initial plan was that we'd keep the news as quiet as we could and get everything organised, and then make some sort of announcement ourselves at some point. I don't think we were going to try and keep it a secret for very long, but we just felt it would probably be best once we'd got our own heads around the situation – then we would do something. But it was almost like a secret that was just impossible to keep, because the crew started to find out, and I think people in the business knew, the record company obviously knew and before long, it was out. There was a delay in making an announcement about, you know, 'this is what we're doing, the band's gonna split' kind of stuff, so it got out there of its own accord. Some so-and-so just leaked it.

NEIL 'TWINK' TINNING There was a leak inquiry. 'Wasn't me.' 'No, I know it wasn't you.' It was meant to be announced on *The Tube* in November '82. They were the first band to do *The Tube*, it was their first episode. That would have been 5 November, but the news went out a lot earlier than that.

Mick Talbot, formerly of Mod group The Merton Parkas, who would go on to co-found Style Council with Paul Weller at the end of 1982. (Steve Rapport/Getty Images)

Right (Erica Echenberg/ Redferns)

'We had a meeting that was only supposed to last half an hour and it ended up being four or five hours. Music was the first point of call but we'd drift off into clothes and films and books and plays. It was almost like a game of chess: "Oh what do you think of the adaptations of Nell Dunn's novels? Have you got Poor Cow? What about Up The Junction? Yeah, have you got the soundtrack? Yeah, the one by Manfred Mann?" Lots of things that were quite niche back then. If you mentioned it and someone had a detailed knowledge of it you knew they were for real. There was no going to the loo and Googling it in 1982.'

MICK TALBOT TO CHRIS CATCHPOLE, *ESQUIRE*, 31 OCTOBER 2020

AUTUMN 1982

SEPTEMBER An estimated 14 per cent of the UK workforce are said to be unemployed | **21 OCTOBER**, Sinn Fein win their first seats in the Northern Ireland Assembly | The UK Government announces that 400,000 council homes have been sold off under the 'right to buy' scheme over the past three years | **2 NOVEMBER** Channel 4 broadcasts for the first time | **22 NOVEMBER** The Who announce their 'farewell' tour in Washington D.C.

6 SEPTEMBER The Jam release 'The Bitterest Pill' EP, reaching number two | **20 SEPTEMBER –1 OCTOBER** The Jam tour the UK | **30 OCTOBER** The split is announced to public | **5 NOVEMBER** The Jam appear on the first episode of *The Tube* | **22 NOVEMBER** The Jam's final single 'Beat Surrender' is released and goes to number one | **25 NOVEMBER** The Jam's Farewell 'Beat Surrender' tour begins.

THE BITTEREST PILL
(I EVER HAD TO SWALLOW)

RICK BUCKLER People often get the wrong idea from 'The Bitterest Pill'.[1] A lot of people think it's about the band splitting up, but the origin of this song paralleled a scenario from an unfortunate medical condition contracted after a clandestine encounter with another woman, and the 'swallowing' of the medicine and having to confess. Whether or not it came from personal experience or not, the play on words worked well.

I always admired Paul for digging deep when he was writing his lyrics; all admiration to Paul for actually spilling that out in a song. That thing about Paul's emotions, and what happened when he actually came to baring his soul? This was the way he did it; he wrote these things down in his lyrics. It seemed to be an emotional outpouring – it's not somebody standing there sobbing and being in pain, you know, but he's actually made something creative out of it and used as fuel. And yet you couldn't get it out of him if you if you sat and spoke to him. He just kept it together, and put it together with a song.

I suppose it's a bit like an act of putting on that character, and playing that part – and nobody is sure whether it's really him or not. I think there's a sort of barrier that songwriters put up so it becomes easier to get all this stuff off your chest in a song. I think Paul was very good at that. I think it was a way of him taking his emotions and channelling them into something much more worthwhile. It was from the soul.

PETER WILSON The idea of 'The Bitterest Pill' is deliberately retro: I see it as in that sixties genre of bittersweet romantic ballad, but with a bit of gritty guitar.

RICK BUCKLER We had Jennie Matthias come and do backing vocals on 'The Bitterest Pill'. She was having success with her own band The Belle Stars and had been doing stuff with Madness. She was going out with Chris Foreman from Madness at the time. Her voice was a nice addition to the record.[2]

JENNIE MATTHIAS Our connection came about because Paolo Hewitt was doing a photo feature for the *Melody Maker* with Paul Weller, and he said, 'we've

got to have another artist on the cover with you.' Paul Weller said, 'I want that girl from The Belle Stars.' I didn't even know him. He's a nice guy! They're all nice guys. I love Rick, he's a good man. He's always doing something for somebody.

GARY CROWLEY That's the other thing about The Jam. If Paul met you, whether you're a girl or a boy, he was always incredibly encouraging – 'how can I help?'. All three of them did that. They'd have young bands supporting them or they'd be name-checking them in interviews. Later with The Style Council, Paul had this revolving door of young musicians as well. I always thought was really, really cool.

JENNIE MATTHIAS After this photo session and interview, Paul called up my record company – he was

Jennie Matthias of The Belle Stars at The Ex Club in Brussels, October 1982. (Gie Knaeps/ Getty Images)

---

[1]*Released on 18 September.*

[2]*Rick Buckler, Ian Snowball,* The Dead Straight Guide to The Jam, *Red Planet, 2017.*

'Weller's written a new Jam song. It's a slow soul number that will use strings and a wailing woman singer. The song is called 'The Bitterest Pill' and Weller's proud of it, proud because for once it has no politics, that it's a love song, proud because it's more dramatic than recent Jam singles.'

MARK COOPER, *RECORD MIRROR*, 17 JULY 1982

a real gentleman – he asked for permission from Stiff Records for me to be on his record, and that was it, hey presto, I'm on the single. And I have to say, he asked me to do a harmony and I didn't even know what a harmony was; I'd only just joined The Belle Stars, I was very green, I was like, 'what's a harmony?!'

So he asked me to do this, and I thought I was bloody rubbish, to be honest, but it taught me a lesson and now I'm amazing at harmonies because of it. He doesn't even know that, but because of that experience, I realised, 'I've got a lot to learn here.' Now I'm really good at harmonies.

I just went in and did it. The Jam were an edgy band, and you do as the Romans do – I was with the Romans, so that's how I did it! Everyone seems to like it, but listening back to it I cringe because I know I could have done a better job – now. But you learn from your mistakes, and that experience was one of the biggest lessons on my journey.

RICK BUCKLER There was a lot going on with 'The Bitterest Pill's single sleeve's front cover. There's a story behind the imagery. It was Vaughn Toulouse on the front cover. I think he was meant to be dressed as some sort of French revolutionary in what appears to be a prison cell. Vaughn was a nice fella, very genuine, who we knew since he played with Department S. They'd had a hit with a song called 'Is Vic There?' in 1980. After Department S he went under the name Main T and had a single out on Paul's Respond label called 'Fickle Public Speaking'. He sadly died in 1991.

Being essentially a ballad, 'The Bitterest Pill' was not a great song in our live set, but it did reach number two in the UK charts – 'The Eye of the Tiger' by Survivor kept 'The Bitterest Pill' from getting to number one. The recording of the B-side track was a real pleasure, as it was something very different style-wise for us. 'Pity Poor Alfie' and 'Fever' are real gems in my book, with fabulous contributions from the brass section, and, in contrast to the A-side, always went down well in our live set.

VALERIE SIEBERT *in* The Quietus[3] If anything could have suggested a future for The Jam, it's the punchy 'Pity Poor Alfie'. It stands out from the rest of the soul numbers and from the group's usual sound, almost big-band-like; yet there's something intrinsically Jam-like about it. Buckler and Foxton are on incredible form here, certainly enough to bring curiosity on what could have come next had they remained a trio.

THE SPLIT IS ANNOUNCED

GARY CROWLEY My memory is that I might have heard from someone at *Melody Maker* just before the announcement was made. They did a press release, which obviously went to all of the music papers. It seemed to happen quite quickly.

MARK ELLEN The readers were mortified when they split up, a bolt out of the blue. We got a ton of letters.

SIMON WELLS[4] With the most loyal fanbase since The Beatles, pulling the plug on the nation's favourite threesome was always going to be an explosive, if risky finale.

PENNIE SMITH I might have been surprised about the split at the time, but you know, a lot of bands break up when they've done what they intended to do originally, they grow away from each other. Bands are primarily blokes exploring the planet together with a similar identity – once they start getting different inputs individually, they grow apart like any relationship.

[3] *Valerie Siebert,* The Quietus, *2012.*

[4] *Simon Wells, 'The Jam: December 11th 1982', Modculture.co.uk, September 2011.*

EDDIE PILLER When it was announced they were splitting up, the front page of my fanzine *Extraordinary Sensations* showed a picture of Paul Weller with the words 'The Bitterest Pill I Ever Had To Swallow' underneath. I wrote a kind of dissection of how surprised at this point we were that The Jam were quitting, but you know, I understood Paul's decision. I think Rick and Bruce didn't, and I know Paul had made his decision some months earlier but didn't tell the others. They were as surprised about it as we were.

NOEL GALLAGHER[5] *in* **Made in Britain, BBC Radio 6 Music** I remember the day of the announcement vividly, because we'd come home from school and we got off the bus and there were some guys that we used to hang out with that were older – and they had the feather-cuts and that – and as we got off the bus, they said, 'The Jam's split up'. I don't want to sound dramatic about it but there were shockwaves through certainly the young kids on our estate. What was left after that? Haircut 100, I think.

RICK BUCKLER There was a weird sort of scenario going on, you know; there we were, quite gentlemanly, acting very professional as we felt we should, the shows were going well, but we were thinking, 'something's not right here. Is Paul simply going to walk out on this?' You know, I always thought he would change his mind.

MAT OSMAN They were really young. I mean, in terms of looking forward I was a baby at 23. It was a brave thing to do, and it must have been incredibly hard for the other two, because they were a once-in-a-generation band. It didn't really matter what they did afterwards; in a way it would be much better to be in a second-division band and split, because then there's a chance that whatever you do next is kind of on a level or bigger than what you did first. I mean, you're never going to be in a band that has that zeitgeisty moment again – even Weller, who has gone on to do amazing things... you're never going to have that sweeping a generation along with you in the same way.

RICK BUCKLER There was a marked moment when the press really shifted their attention onto Paul, 'what are you gonna do next? What's happening now?' Which we never got involved in; they just didn't come to us for that.

Above: The Tube (Rex Shutterstock)

Right: The Tube, 5 November 1982. (Kevin Cummins /Getty Images)

'GET ME OUT OF HERE, MILES...' THE FIRST EPISODE OF *THE TUBE*

RICK BUCKLER An appearance on *The Tube* was offered to us, ironically to help launch the new TV show on 5 November 1982, with Jools Holland and Paula Yates hosting.[6]

JAMIE TELFORD I only heard we were doing *The Tube* on the bus on the way there... 'oh yes, we are going to Newcastle to appear on a TV programme.' It was the first episode of *The Tube* and The Jam were going to grace it with their first – and last – appearance.

RICK BUCKLER Paul had tried other avenues apart from music, but most fell upon stoney ground. The bands he did try to invest in and help did not have the success he hoped they would, and publishing poetry failed as well. Talk of a record company was short-lived... it was as if he was not sure what to try next. We saw conflicting tales of direction and non-direction. I think John thought that the revenue was going to dry up. I'm all for trying new ideas but they all seemed badly conceived, he appeared almost lost. On the other hand, it wasn't a bad way to dispose of his Jam proceeds.

---

[5]*BBC Radio 6 Music documentary,* The Jam: Made in Britain, *2002. Producers: Frank Wilson and Dave Barber.*

[6]*The inaugural episode also featured appearances from Sunderland punk group The Toy Dolls and Heaven 17.*

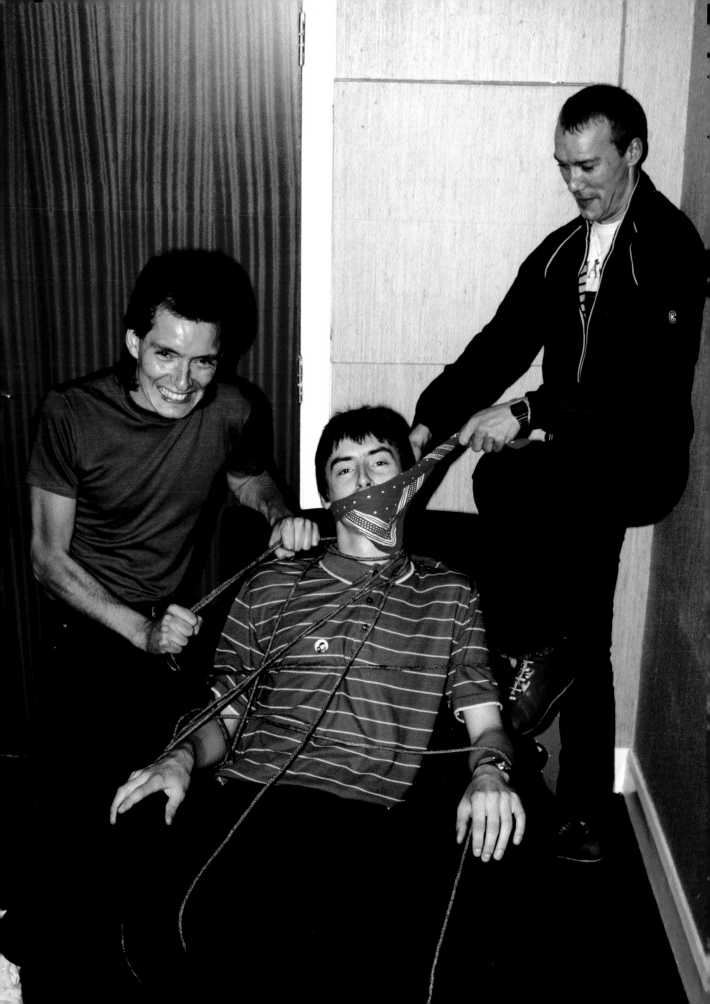

Muriel Gray, The Tube, 5 November 1982: *'Now, most people know that The Jam are splitting up at the end of this year, and indeed the television appearance they'll be making tonight in about half an hour's time is probably going to be the last live television appearance they make. Now a big question that everybody's asking is: 'what is Paul Weller going to do next?' Let's burst into the dressing room, catch him in his vest and ask him. Hello?*
Paul Weller: *Go away.*
Muriel Gray: *And it's Paul Weller! Now Paul, what about the split? What are you going to do now?*
Paul Weller: *I'm not sure yet, I don't think any of us have got any definite plans.*
Muriel Gray: *Well, you've been involved in a whole lot of other things apart from the music, haven't you? For instance, there's the record company ...*
Paul Weller: *It's funny you should mention that. We've got this one group called The Questions who've got a single out at the moment called 'Work And Play'.*
Muriel Gray: *Are they going to do an album?*
Paul Weller: *Well, that won't be until next year, we're trying to get some singles off the ground first. No one seems to be buying the records yet.*
Muriel Gray: *Oh well, maybe with your name behind them, eh? [laughs] The other thing you've been doing is fanzines, and you write poetry too...*
Paul Weller: *We've done some poetry fanzines and ... we've got a book of poetry coming out by Aidan Cant, a local Geordie lad, and loads of other things lined up.*

JAMIE TELFORD I remember on set at *The Tube*, being with Paul while meeting the producer Malcolm Gerrie. I chirped up with some irrelevance and Malcolm Gerrie just went, 'who are you, mate?' Paul just laughed. Strange event, smallish studio but The Jam got the red carpet treatment.

It was Muriel Gray and Jools Holland's first time as presenters, and they looked a bit lost. It was quite chaotic. I remember Sting backstage shouting to his manager Miles Copeland, 'Get me out of here, Miles.'

RICK BUCKLER What made *The Tube* attractive for us was the fact that we could play a short live set, unusual for an in-house television production. A brass section was hired and Jamie Telford, who had been with us on our live shows, on keyboards. Caron Wheeler and Claudia Fontaine – aka Afrodiziak – were on backing vocals.

Rick: We all thought tying Paul up was a weird idea for a photo shoot, but played along, trying not to be too rough. (Neil Matthews/Rex Shutterstock)

I thought Afrodiziak were fabulous.[7] Caron had started out in a three-piece called Brown Sugar but after this fell through she teamed up with Claudia Fontaine to form the duo that was Afrodiziak. They did session work and they got our attention and we invited them in to come on the road. Caron later went on to join Soul II Soul, who were hugely successful in the later eighties. (In fact, I still kick myself because, in the last days of The Jam's final tour, Caron asked if I wanted to be the drummer in a band she was forming. I declined!)

Back to *The Tube*, both Caron and Claudia were very excited and pushed the boat out, having had matching outfits made just for the occasion. Dennis Munday travelled up to Newcastle for the day to be with us, and despite everything, there was a very good atmosphere in the studio and even Paul could be seen smiling on occasion.

JAMIE TELFORD There was the horn section and two girl backing singers, Caron Wheeler and Claudia Fontaine.

---

[7] *Rick Buckler, Ian Snowball,* The Dead Straight Guide to The Jam, *Red Planet, 2017.*

*From the set
at* The Tube.
*(All photos Rex
Shutterstock)*

FINAL TOUR

RICK BUCKLER It had become usual for us to put together a UK tour, finishing off with a Christmas party for all who had worked with us throughout the year. Dates were already in the process of being organised as early as June, and signed commitments made: it did seem like the final tour had started in the summer and went on until the show in Brighton.

The major problem we had was that we still owed product, mainly one more album, to Polydor, and it was obvious that we were not going to be able to record and deliver an original album with any enthusiasm, especially from Paul.

It was suggested that a live album was an easy way out of this contractual commitment. Unfortunately

Dig the New Breed was hastily put together and signed off without too much involvement from us, to be released a day before our last concert at Brighton, on 11 December 1982. With respect to The Jam's catalogue, I think now that the album was too short and would have better served The Jam's legacy if it had been a double album.

I always thought that almost any song from any of our albums could have been a single, the strength of Paul's songwriting threw up many great songs that were left waiting to be discovered on an album's listings, and did not gain full attention. For a final album, there was plenty of recorded live material to choose from but the production was hurried and lacked the care and strength that came with the later release of *Live Jam*, released more than a decade later in October 1993.

JAMIE TELFORD I did a couple of tours with them, so I was on the live album. But it was mixed so weirdly, I never listened to it.

I got called earlier in the year to work with the group because we had the same music publisher at the time, and the booking agent knew they were looking for a keyboard player. They were rehearsing up in Golders Green and... I mean, I wasn't the biggest Jam fan, and I was there with no music, and not having listened to the tracks. They were like: 'All right, let's go!' And I was thinking: 'Now... what am I supposed to do with this?' I could see them looking at me going, 'OK...' But it got better.

I was more for improvising across the top of the stuff than sort of learning the notes, but obviously, I learned the notes for things like 'Town Called Malice' and riffs and things like that. I wasn't absolutely brilliant at the time, and I've subsequently got a lot better, but they put up with me, and I got into the groove of it.

The dad, John Weller, kind of ran the band. The whole thing was all around Paul and his dad. He was pretty sharp. I remember being a bit bemused: I hadn't been exposed to the whole 'Cockney' thing before; I was living in Edinburgh at the time, so obviously, I'm 'Scotch'. I used to get 'yer Scotch git', 'Hamish'...

I think it was quite good for them to have other musicians there with them on tour. I mean, I was just a voyager along for the ride, and I really enjoyed the experience: it was great for me, and it really woke me up to a lot of things. But it was very intense. They wouldn't have said much about what was going on, but nobody was very happy.

(Stephen O'Connell/ Alamy)

Barry Cain, Flexipop, 1982: You're upsetting a hell of a lot of people by splitting the band. Doesn't that concern you at all?

Paul Weller: Sure – but you've got to put yourself first. Look, if I carried on doing what I've been doing over the last few years – touring, releasing albums, choosing the singles – I'd go mad. I need time to get out of this whole insular set up. We're not public property. Never have been and never will be.

Maybe it is a selfish attitude. But at the same time they are important reasons to help me keep sane... if we didn't give a fuck about it and decided we were only in it for the money, we could plough on forever. But The Jam has always been more than that. Right from the start, it has always transcended just being a group and just being music. It's much, much stronger.

PAUL WELLER *to Phil Sutcliffe,* **MOJO**[16] There was a lot of tension, which was great for us live, because it had this snarl to it. But offstage it was a fuckin' pain in the arse.

EDDIE PILLER When they announced that they were splitting, it caused an incredible rush on tickets – it was always hard to get a ticket for Jam gigs anyway, but that made it very difficult. There were a lot of incidents of people climbing in through windows and kicking backdoors down, just getting in however they could. There'd always been some of that at Jam gigs anyway but that last tour, it was almost a hysterical response from Jam fans.

RICK BUCKLER More and more shows were being added, and it just got embarrassing: 'No, no, we've got to stop. We can't keep doing this.' We could have kept adding more and more shows because there was no lack of appetite for buying tickets for them. I mean, that was the view: that the band were going to be no more at the end of the year and this was the last chance.

A lot of people went to several shows and travelled around the country, and as the year moved on from the summertime through to the end, there were all sorts of strange feelings going on, not only in the band, but from the audience as well.

JAMIE TELFORD It was incredibly heightened. I've never really experienced anything quite like it. I'd never been on such serious big tours before, where the audience went absolutely mad. I mean, they really were huge at that point; it would have

been as near to The Beatles as anything you could get. But knowing that it was the end, that enhanced the level of mania, definitely. You'd have people weeping, it got hysterical at times. It was quite powerful.

BRUCE FOXTON[17] It was a real rollercoaster. I don't know if we just thought we'd got this final point to prove or something, but we all played brilliantly and yeah, mixed emotions. We'd still meet fans after the show and they'd all be in tears, 'why are you calling it a day?', and I'm in tears on the other side: 'I don't know! I don't know.'

NEIL 'TWINK' TINNING Some of the fans were really in bits. It's hard to think what music was like in '82. I mean, there were only three channels on the TV, bands would either get *Top of the Pops*, if you're lucky *Old Grey Whistle Test*, or children's TV on a Saturday morning. No internet; it was a completely different world to what we're living in now.

JAMIE TELFORD People were going mad, people were waiting for the tour bus, there'd be people screaming at them. They'd play the gigs and people would go bonkers – and I've never really seen that before in the same way. It was mental. It was absolutely mental.

A few of the shows were incredible. There was a show in Leeds where the stage was going up and down about three foot as we played; it was like being on the sea, you know? Wow. And the crowd were crazy. I mean, they were crazy. Same in Glasgow.

---

[16]*Phil Sutcliffe, 'Paul Weller: The* MOJO *Interview',* MOJO, *2004.*

[17]*Gary Crowley interview with Bruce Foxton and Rick Buckler for DVD release* From The Jam – A First Class Return, *Invisible Hands Music, 2008.2004. The Jam, Paul Weller.*

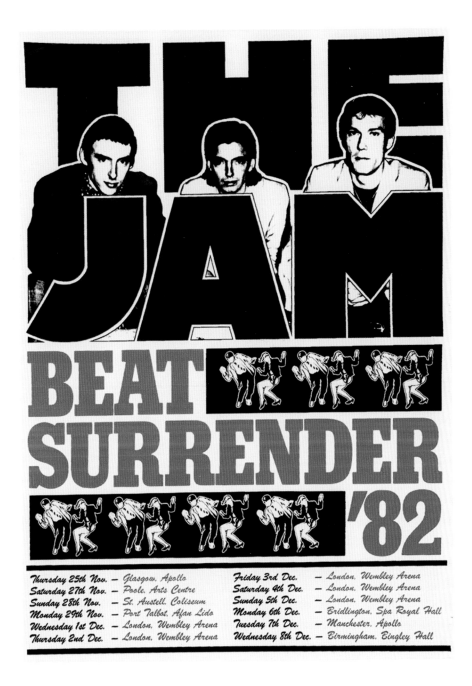

THE JAM
BEAT SURRENDER '82

Thursday 25th Nov. — Glasgow. Apollo
Saturday 27th Nov. — Poole. Arts Centre
Sunday 28th Nov. — St. Austell. Coliseum
Monday 29th Nov. — Port Talbot. Afan Lido
Wednesday 1st Dec. — London. Wembley Arena
Thursday 2nd Dec. — London. Wembley Arena
Friday 3rd Dec. — London. Wembley Arena
Saturday 4th Dec. — London. Wembley Arena
Sunday 5th Dec. — London. Wembley Arena
Monday 6th Dec. — Bridlington. Spa Royal Hall
Tuesday 7th Dec. — Manchester. Apollo
Wednesday 8th Dec. — Birmingham. Bingley Hall

The good thing about playing the Glasgow Apollo was that they had a very high stage, so the crowd couldn't get near you – which was safer because they were mental.

People revered them and hung on every word – even though every word can be prosaic. There were a lot of intense guys taking notes, and they were obsessed with the lyrics as well. They'd be like, 'Paul, Paul, what do you mean by this?' He was always good with fans, he always had a bit of time for them. I saw the other side of him as well, but when you're young there's that kind of feeling that you are absolutely right.

It's hard when you're 24 to have that kind of poise, and to be that popular. It's really stressful. For me, I went into it not knowing much about them or their material: I wasn't that bothered by The Jam, but I actually came away realising Paul was a great songwriter. Some people have got it from an early age and some people haven't, and he had it, you know?

'Like Rick Buckler, Bruce may be facing the group's retirement with reluctance, but both of them play with blatant determination to go down with all musical guns blazing – almost as though they've resolved to cram another eight years' energy into as many single concerts.'

PAUL DU NOYER, *NME*, 11 DECEMBER 1982

An overexcited fan is shown the door at the 3 December Wembley Arena show. (Pete Still/ Redferns)

I liked the best. The guys at the drum factory had a hell of a time making the long shells and keeping them straight. I loved them when they turned up at the rehearsal studio and just had to keep all three, but there was no way to mount them – so Wally Miller, my drum tech, devised a way of linking them together and suspending them on two cymbal stands. It was a monster to set-up and tricky to play, as the distance from the snare to the first tom was quite a jump. One of the other downsides was that I was hidden behind this cliff of drums. I had the whole kit fitted with contact mics inside the shells to cut down on the forest of mic stands that usually surround a drum kit, and it made setting up a little easier. It was draped and hidden with a black cloth during the support act. Wally would remove the drape about five minutes before we hit the stage and the atmosphere from the crowd would always go up several notches. Amazingly, the Great White has survived to this day and is often used as a centrepiece at Jam exhibitions.

PAUL DU NOYER *in* NME, *review of Wembley arena* On the first night of the final five shows at Wembley, they start with 'Start!' and the crowd barriers are rushed, and the whole event soars to a level of instant intensity from which it never descends until the very end. How do they hope to maintain such impact, such energy, over all the farewell dates to come? I can only wonder. What's clearest, though, is that the fact of The Jam playing Wembley means this thing has got as big as it should ever be allowed to get. The Jam don't make megaband music; they're not about grand gestures and heroic poses, dimly viewed from a seat two miles away. It's only the unique nature of the event, with all its attendant emotional charge, that saves the band's onstage graft from getting lost in space.

JAMIE TELFORD I do remember when we were at Wembley, Paul decided he was going to play 'That's Entertainment', which we'd never rehearsed. I hadn't got a clue what I was playing. He started it off, and I'm going 'yep, got this,' and then, 'oh no, the change... I don't know what the fuck it is.'

So I kept playing but I was turning the sound down on the Hammond to keep it very quiet because I just didn't want to fuck it up. But as I turned it down to keep it quiet, the guy on the mixing desk was turning it up because he couldn't hear me. And then Paul was turning around at me going, 'What the fuck are you doing, Hamish?'

It's one of these embarrassing moments where we hadn't rehearsed it, and I had no clue what I was doing, but I was giving it a go anyway. 'That's Entertainment'... it's not quite as easy to follow that song as it would sound. We got away with it, it was just a fight.

RICK BUCKLER To be honest, I didn't really take much notice of what was going on on that side of things. I had me own headaches, didn't I?

GARY CROWLEY On those last dates, there was a kind of coolness backstage. Bruce would be over there – he had a lovely wife, Pat, she would have been around. Rick would have been over there, and obviously Paul would have been with Gill, his girlfriend... it didn't feel very positive. I mean, I didn't see anyone throwing their toys out the pram but it wasn't harmonious. There was no bitching, it just seemed a bit deflated, like, 'the end is nigh' kind of feeling.

JAMIE TELFORD But the whole thing for me, it was really good. It was exciting, and though I never realised it at the time, it was interesting to be a part of their peak, and a fly on the wall at the same time.

Strangely enough, I felt after I'd done it, I thought maybe I should just stop because, you know, it couldn't get much better.

IN CONCERT ✚ **BIG COUNTRY** SOLD OUT

DECEMBER 1ST to 5TH 7.15 P.M.

NEW ALBUM **Dig The New Breed** OUT NEXT WEEK

Five nights at Wembley Arena! (Phil Dent/Redferns)

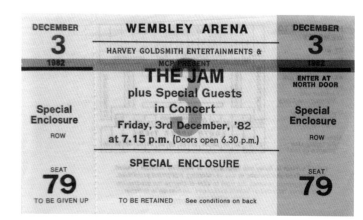

DECEMBER **3** 1982	**WEMBLEY ARENA**		DECEMBER **3** 1982
	HARVEY GOLDSMITH ENTERTAINMENTS & MCP PRESENT		
	THE JAM		ENTER AT NORTH DOOR
	plus Special Guests		
Special Enclosure	in Concert		Special Enclosure
ROW	Friday, 3rd December, '82		ROW
	at **7.15 p.m.** (Doors open 6.30 p.m.)		
	SPECIAL ENCLOSURE		
SEAT **79**			SEAT **79**
TO BE GIVEN UP	TO BE RETAINED See conditions on back		

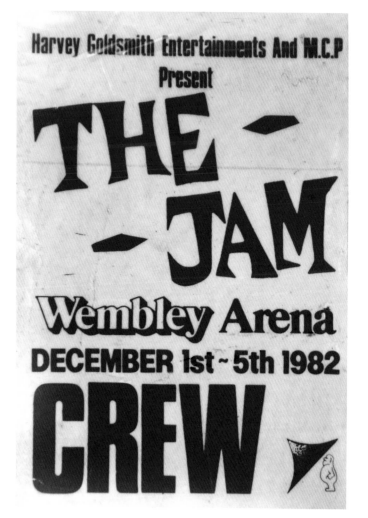

Harvey Goldsmith Entertainments And M.C.P
Present
THE JAM
Wembley Arena
DECEMBER 1st ~ 5th 1982
CREW

*Wembley Arena
(Phil Dent/
Redferns)*

'Weller came on at the evening's start with a clipped, "Hello and welcome to the Red Cow..."' [4]

[4] *A reference to the Hammersmith pub rock – and subsequently punk rock – venue played by The Jam in their formative years. Quote from Paul du Noyer's live review for NME of The Jam at Wembley Arena, December 1982.*

FROM HOMETOWN
TO MOD-TOWN

SIMON WELLS[5] It seemed the band had thrown everything in on this tour. Brighton, though, was just one gig too many; especially after their previous appearance a few days before at Guildford. To all intents and purposes, Guildford was the full-circle gig: those present recall an emotional night where the band played their hearts and souls out to fans, friends and family. As a band they'd mentally worked towards Guildford as being the final hurdle, making a further gig an emotionally redundant affair.

RICK BUCKLER The Guildford show had a very personal buzz to it; when I was growing up, I saw my first shows there, and I'd dream of what it would be like to play there, what happened after the band disappeared behind the stage doors. The fantastic mystery was nothing to shout about in reality. The dressing room was as plain as any other backstage area. All the real excitement could be seen out in the packed auditorium, the house lights were still up and all I could see were the heads of the buzzing crowd

moving like a boiling stew. Playing to such a crowd was what it was all about for me. I could not wait to get out there.

EDDIE PILLER For me, I went to about ten to twelve gigs on that tour, and I think the most exciting gig was Guildford, which I remember very well. It was about a week before Brighton and we felt it was important because it was a bit smaller. The doors got kicked in, security got bundled over and the place was absolutely heaving. It was like their final hometown gig. In my head that was always the last gig, and I'd forgotten that Brighton came after it, because it was such an anti-climax compared to Guildford.

SIMON WELLS[6] The Jam were at number one in both album and singles charts, and so a Saturday night at Brighton's Conference Centre (reportedly Weller's favourite venue at the time) had been slotted in to satisfy the final demand. I think it was Mike Read on BBC Radio 1 who announced it. To many, it seemed fitting that the band chose Brighton for their last hurrah. Brighton will always be a mod town.

[5]*Simon Wells, 'The Jam: 11th December 1982', Modculture.co.uk, September 2011.*

[6]*Simon Wells, 'The Jam: 11th December 1982', Modculture.co.uk, September 2011.*

The Brighton Centre, Brighton, 22 September 1982. (Erica Echenberg/ Redferns)

When you hear of 'last' concerts, you conjure up images and expectations that a band can't simply hope to achieve. Nonetheless as I hadn't attended The Beatles' last soiree at Candlestick Park in 1966, nor Cream's farewell fandango at the Albert Hall, I was sure as hell going to be at The Jam's (my generation's Beatles) last bash. The anticipation the few days before the gig was unbearable.

MAT OSMAN I was a massive, massive fan. I read everything I could about them in the music press, but I never saw them until that last gig.

SIMON WELLS[7] It was miserably wet and overcast; not unusual for the South Coast in December. The Centre had actually put on their hoarding 'The Jam's Last Concert' (as if we didn't know!). We managed to miss the soundcheck (something that had become a ritualised matinee of Jam gigs) but were informed that it had been a miserable affair, Weller and Foxton barely communicating with each other.

MAT OSMAN I didn't really have any context for it, I don't think I'd quite processed what a big deal it was. None of the bands I was interested in had ever split up before. And Paul was so young, I just assumed that whatever he did next would be 'the next Jam'.

I don't think I realised the enormity of it until I saw people at the gig, especially people who were slightly older, for whom it was a really emotional moment in terms of... I guess the end of adolescence for a lot of people. People slightly older than me for whom I think The Jam had been a huge part of their identity. I was too young for it to feel like an ending in the way it obviously did for people around me.

SIMON WELLS[8] There were hordes of people outside literally begging for tickets and handing over extortionate sums to the parasitic touts that flocked around the venue. I clearly recall too, a large posse of skinheads milling around.

EDDIE PILLER We travelled by coach and were greeted when we arrived by quite a lot of skinheads, who were waiting to attack young mod kids; I remember we had quite a big fight on the seafront against the skinheads. A friend of mine got hit in the face with a hammer. I got in to the gig through a window.

NEIL 'TWINK' TINNING I'm pretty sure it was Brighton when Rick got locked out of the gig. There's a backdoor way from the Grand Hotel into the Conference Centre, and I went that way with Weller and Bruce. I didn't know where Rick was. He was banging on the front door, 'Let me in, let me in!' The fans were all around him saying, 'It's Rick Buckler!'

RICK BUCKLER It was stupid of me to dawdle behind but Paul's henchman just shut the doors behind him, so when I came around the corner a second later I was too late. I had to walk around to the front entrance to try and get in that way, but the door staff wouldn't let me in. 'The doors are not open yet, mate. You will have to wait.' Despite the crowd behind me shouting, 'but he's in the band, there won't be a show without him,' they would not let me in.

'OK, where's your ticket?'

'I don't have one!'

'Stage pass then.'

I didn't have that either.

The penny soon dropped as he looked at me, then looked at a large poster inside the foyer and then back at me. He finally opened the door and let me in.

SIMON WELLS[9] The ground floor area was standing and the three facing tiers were seated; many people had tried to gate-crash the arena floor and, obviously, aware that this might happen, extra security staff were placed on the doors to prevent this. It was no surprise then, Jam fans being what they were (are?), that those with seating tickets simply leapt the 12–15 foot drop from the gallery and hastily buried themselves in the crowd. Once the lights went down it was like a sea of mod lemmings. One enterprising mod even used his Parka to lever his mates down onto the floor.

EDDIE PILLER I managed to get on the stage. I got thrown off by Kenny Wheeler who gave me a couple of sharp digs on the way down into the orchestra pit.

SIMON WELLS[10] One of the supports was Apocalypse, a band from Weller's 'Jamming' label-stable. I didn't think much of them – nor did a lot of the crowd – but it was brave move to put them on that night.

---

[7]*Simon Wells, 'The Jam: 11th December 1982', Modculture.co.uk, September 2011.*

[8]*Ibid*

[9]*Simon Wells, 'The Jam: 11th December 1982', Modculture. co.uk, September 2011.*

[10]*Ibid*

Previous spread and this page: soundcheck and before gig. (Justin Thomas)

THE BRIGHTON CENTRE

SATURDAY, 11th DECEMBER, 1982
at 7.30 p.m.

M.C.P.
PRESENT

THE JAM PLUS
GUESTS

WEST BALCONY

C 43   £4.50

Skyline RESTAURANT

(Magnificent Sea View)
Open two hours prior to most performances
Reservations: Telephone 203130

Neither the Council or their officers accept any responsibility for any loss or damage (howsoever caused or sustained) to any property whatsoever brought on to these premises.
Tickets cannot be exchanged or refunded.

The taking of unauthorised photographs during the artiste's live performance is a breach of the Copyright Act 1956. Cameras being used in defiance of this regulation will be removed to the cloakroom for the duration of the performance. The Management may also exercise the right to expose film if so requested by the artiste.

(Mauro Carraro/ Mirrorpix)

NEIL 'TWINK' TINNING There was a guy called Dave Liddle, who was Paul Weller's roadie, or 'first among equals', if you want to call it that. Dave used to wind people up, so the rest of the crew got together and said, 'right, we're gonna have him on the last gig.' And the crew actually tied him up by his feet and put them up on the truss rods at the last gig. He was dangling by his feet on the lighting rig. So that happened. But overall, it was just very sad. I think everybody tried to put a good face on it but you could tell... it was like a bereavement.

RICK BUCKLER We always used to stay in the Grand, which was next door to the venue. Normally, under any circumstances – under all circumstances apart from this particular one – we'd be getting on the bus the next morning to go somewhere else. Or if it was the end of tour, we'd still be getting on the bus, but getting taken to our various homes. But this time it just wasn't the case. It was just, 'right. That's it. Make your own way home.'

There were fans hanging around outside the hotel, and neither the fans nor myself could find anything to say to each other. That was a bit strange. In the past that wouldn't have been the case. That was the one day in the whole of The Jam's career that was just empty. I think that's probably the best word for it.

NEIL 'TWINK' TINNING I remember coming back in the car from the last gig with Rick and Lesley: you could cut the atmosphere with a knife. It was a very, very sombre car journey. I think it was the next day or the day after that Rick wanted to copy the video of the last gig, the one we'd taken from the sound desk. I managed to do that. 'What's it for?' 'I'll tell you later.'

It ended up him, Lesley and me, back in the car – I didn't even know where we were going – and we went to a hospital. There was one Jam fan who was dying of leukaemia who couldn't come to the gig. So Rick took the video of the last gig to this lad who was dying. It was around Christmas time, and Lesley and I went with him to the hospital, but Rick went into the ward by himself with the video and the idea was that they were going to play him the video of the last gig because he couldn't make it. It was such a sad time for him personally – and not only him. I just thought that spoke volumes.

After they split up, I didn't pick up my camera for twenty years. I think it's more to do with my mental health: I was photographing for the biggest band and then coming off that... it was horrendous. Then in early January 1983, all of my photographic gear got stolen at a Madness gig. All of my film was in the bag, including film of the last Jam gig. Everything got stolen, and I thought, 'Oh, I can't be doing with this.'

*Previous page
and right: The
final curtain.
(Mauro Carraro/
Mirrorpix)*

*Overleaf: Fans
gather for the
farewell concert
at the Brighton
Centre. (Janette
Beckman/
Getty Images)*

NEW YEAR 1983

(Erica Echenberg/ Redferns)

1 JANUARY The year begins with Renée and Renato (still) at number one with 'Save Your Love' | Breakfast television franchise TV-am broadcasts for the first time on **1 FEBRUARY** | **8 FEBRUARY** racehorse Shergar is stolen by an armed gang | In March, the compact disc goes on sale for the first time in the UK | **11 MARCH** The Style Council releases first single 'Speak Like a Child', featuring Tracie Young on backing vocals.

GARY CROWLEY Paul had his studio and it soon became a hub in a way, a place to go. The Style Council had obviously started recording by then and there was more socialising going on. Paul also lived just behind the studio so it was easy to see him; you'd call up or he'd call up, 'what are you up to?' Word would get around and we'd meet up with so and so. There was a little gang of us: Paul, obviously, Paolo Hewitt – he and Paul got very, very tight towards the end of The Jam – Paul had asked Paolo to write the 'Beat Surrender' tour programme. Then there was Pete Barrett, and Simon Halfon who did the sleeve work for *Snap*[1], the 'best of' album.

So that was the gang, and we would meet there, or there was a couple of coffee shops or pubs where we'd meet, and we'd talk invariably about music and what we were listening to. With The Style Council there was more hanging out, going to clubs, there was a lot more of that. Bruce and Rick, you know, I didn't see them socially. They were both living outside of London, as well, so I didn't really see them as much.

RICK BUCKLER The other thing was that myself and Bruce didn't really have a great deal of money to start splashing around and doing the sort of things which might have helped. That was another weird thing: you suddenly start taking stock of your situation and you realise, 'we did all this, we had all this success and what did we actually get for it?' That tends to pile on more emotional pressure, you know, the lack of any sort of finances. It was another whammy that we had to deal with.

But, you know, I was 28 years old, still relatively young, and I knew that I just had to get on with things. The world doesn't stop turning all of a sudden – you might have felt like it had, but it doesn't, so there was that to deal with. There was a lot going on in that period which was stressful. Anybody, whoever you are, it doesn't matter whether you're a pop star or a suit or you work at the plastic factory, it doesn't matter. It's all the same.

Then you come across this thing of what people expect you to do next, the sort of expectations about what you should be doing. And, you know, that is a terrible expression: 'you should be doing this'. There were people saying, 'you should do this, you should do that. This should happen, this should be going on,' but a lot of things are easier said than done, especially from outsiders. And so it all comes at you. 'How are you going to sort out all these other problems?'

Because the immediate thing is that you want to get yourself back on track, back to where you were a year previously. And it's almost impossible to do.

For my part, I soon came to the conclusion that I wanted to put a band together and go on the road, so I started that process. John Weller had assured me that after settling a few bills that our share of what was left in the band's account would soon be released: these were much-needed funds for me. The first thing I did was to look for a songwriter; I contacted Dennis Munday and he was very helpful. When I next asked John what was happening with our money I was shocked to learn that the account was now empty. All of it had gone. I thought, 'well, hang on a second...'

It became obvious to me that, because John didn't know which way things were gonna go after the band split, I think he collected in as much money as he possibly could. John just didn't know what was going to happen to Paul's career. For my part, I did move on and form Time UK with Jimmy Edwards in 1983. He had been recommended by Dennis Munday and had some good songs ready to go, and he had worked behind the scenes with Sham 69 with their material.

Danny Kustow from Tom Robinson Band was on guitar, Nick South on bass, who seemed to have played with everybody from Yoko to Sniff 'n' the Tears, a very accomplished bass player. We also had Ray Simone on rhythm guitar. It didn't take long for us to be on the road. I found this period very hard financially, as myself and Bruce were having our royalties blocked by John Weller, so money was very tight. We did eventually force John's hand to have our royalties paid direct to us, something he should have done when he was no longer the manager of The Jam.

I think the most upsetting thing was the aftermath of what happened in 1983: there was a lot of backlash from John about Bruce and I, with him referring to us as 'hangers-on'. And I thought, 'what? Really? Come on, we've played our part. There's no real need for any of this.' I don't think there was bad feeling from me and Bruce as such, we just thought some of the things that were said afterwards were unfair and completely unwarranted.

PAUL WELLER *to Phil Sutcliffe,* **MOJO**[2] You get so self-obsessed. Then you need someone – and it can be yourself – saying, 'Remember where you come from, kid, cos you can always end up back there'. Which I nearly did. I'd lost a lot of my audience. The Style

[1] *Released 14 October 1983 (Polydor).*

[2] *Phil Sutcliffe, 'Paul Weller: The* MOJO *Interview', MOJO, September 2004.*

(Steve Rapport/
Getty Images)

Barry Cain, Flexipop, 1982: *Can you honestly say now you've split up you'll remain friends with Rick and Bruce?*
Paul Weller: *When you've worked with people for ten years you're bound to.*
Barry Cain: *But people work in jobs for that length of time, build up close relationships with their workmates yet when they leave they never set eyes on them again. Doesn't it worry you that that might happen?*
Paul Weller: *I haven't thought about it.*

Council's humour was too cliquey, the ideas were too introverted, it was all born out of this little mad vision of mine. People couldn't see it and because of that I was building up my defences: "If you don't like it, fuck it!"
Phil Sutcliffe What was your mad vision?
Paul Weller I don't know. I don't know where my head was.
PS Were you becoming some kind of art snob?
PW I was becoming a complete fuckin' wanker. I'm right and that's it, bang!

RICK BUCKLER My memories of it were that Paul had almost turned into a sort of Val Doonican character. You think, 'hang on, this is not the same angry young guy, with all this passion, that we've grown up with.' Musically speaking, it didn't have a great deal of strength. I think Paul wanted to be like a Steve Marriott soul singer; it might have been an ambition of his but it's not really him. It was like a mix of the New Romantics and the Cafe Society and the big soul singer-songwriter – obviously Paul was a big fan of Marvin Gaye and the Motown stuff. But he would have been much better off, I think, if he'd have stuck to his own style of doing things and try not trying to be something else.

GARY CROWLEY I think Paul could have just felt, 'what we've done is absolutely amazing. And what the three of us achieved is amazing, but I don't want to keep on doing the same thing.' The word 'passionate' is overused, but it really meant everything to him; he was very passionate about the band, and very proud of what they'd achieved. And he's really proud of the fact that people still look back on it and say, 'wow, Jesus, how good was that?' And, it never went down.

RICK BUCKLER To this day there are Jam fans and Paul Weller fans. For myself, I saw little emerging from The Style Council that could hold a light to the songs that Paul had written with The Jam, either lyrically or musically. Maybe he was

hunting for a new direction and in someways he still is.

This thing about the reasons he left the band just didn't seem to add up to the reality on the ground. I think he was probably massaging his own problems. I think a lot of it was probably stress, from his point of view. There was something going on which he wasn't dealing with particularly well. I mean, I haven't spoken to Paul since 1983, so I really don't know what his view is these days on it. It probably doesn't matter. There's obviously no undoing any of that.

Bruce and I felt it was very unfair when, later on, Paul started saying things like, 'we were never friends anyway'. We thought, 'Whoa, where'd that come from?' It seemed like a childish thing to do after the fact. I'm not absolutely sure what all that was about.

He made a point of staying away from myself and Bruce in the years after we split up. I remember Bruce telling me once that he was in Chris Parry's office in 1983, because Parry was obviously the guy who signed us and worked for Polydor Records. Bruce had some business with him.

When Bruce turned up at Chris Parry's office, he was actually on the phone to Paul. He said, 'I've got Bruce here, he just walked in the door. Do you want a word?' And he wouldn't. He wouldn't even say hello, you know? It was really odd because we – myself and Bruce – kept in contact, we go out every now and again and have lunch with their respective other halves and stuff. But staying in touch with Paul was just like 'no'. He just didn't want to go there. We were completely shut out of his bubble.

We'd seen him do that before with other people, girlfriends. Steve Brookes[3] was completely shut off as well. But we thought this is a bit strong, because we'd spent the last ten years pretty much in each other's pockets. But that was the way that that was. Maybe that's why Paul just wanted to say, 'right, I'm finishing it on December 11th and now I'm not talking to you.'

---

[3]*Founding Jam guitarist.*

Mick Talbot and Paul Weller in The Style Council's 'Long Hot Summer' video. (Steve Rapport/Getty Images)

Even in later years, journalists would find him a bit of a sticky character, because he would always tell them off, 'I don't want to talk about The Jam, I want to talk about what I'm doing now.' And you can understand that to a certain degree. But you can't deny it. For some reason, he spent a long time trying to distance himself from The Jam, either personally with me and Bruce, or by not talking about it or not playing the songs live on stage. I don't know. It's difficult to equate exactly what was going on in that respect, but whatever it was, I think it all stemmed from whatever was in his mind in 1982.

There's obviously a lot of people who've have analysed all of this – including myself in some ways, because I get asked it a lot: 'What happened? What went wrong?' And then obviously the other thing is, 'Is there any chance of the band getting back together again?' And you think, 'Well, actually, I don't think so.'

DENNIS MUNDAY I think they stopped at the right time – at the top. The Jam have had a bigger impact than The Clash, even The Sex Pistols. The Sex Pistols knocked the doors down and they did what they did, but it was short-lived. Forty years later, people still talk about The Jam and the influence of The Jam. They've got one of the best songwriters in the country, and the band... Rick and Bruce were a tremendous rhythm section.

You know, everyone says, 'if only The Beatles had carried on,' but you don't know... you've only got to look at the way Paul McCartney went and Lennon went... When you stop at your peak, you have a bigger impact.

NEIL 'TWINK' TINNING The reason we're still talking about them today, in my opinion, is because of

the split. And even if they did get back together again – which I don't think would ever happen – it wouldn't be the same.

GARY CROWLEY I mean, it's not many people who walk away from a band on the back of five nights at Wembley Arena, a number one album, and three or four back-to-back number one singles. The chutzpah of the guy to do that.

NOEL GALLAGHER[4] When you look back on it now, it was the ultimate smart move, splitting up this band right at the peak of their success. I wish I had the guts to do that at Knebworth.

MAT OSMAN The minute Weller feels pinned down, either by the press or by himself, he immediately takes on something else, and it's incredible to watch the last few years of his career – he's still doing it. It's really interesting to watch him and Nick Cave for the last few years, both of them just not doing what you're supposed to do at that 'elder statesman' stage of your career, which is just, 'right, I've got my style...' Both of them are saying, 'I can do basically anything I want now' – and they do it.

GARY CROWLEY Weller's dedication is absolutely total, which I think makes him unique. It's all about the art and his music, and his kind of belief in the power of it. As for The Jam, it never got old, it never got depressing. They went out like The Beatles. It was pure. It was never soiled. The power of The Jam has never, ever, ever diminished.

[4]*BBC Radio 6 Music documentary,* The Jam: Made in Britain, *2002. Producers: Frank Wilson and Dave Barber.*

The final word, from Rick Buckler

_Hindsight is certainly a wonderful
thing. To look back and talk about
The Jam splitting in a very romantic
way and say that it was about just
'moving on' when that is what was
going to happen eventually anyway
is one thing, but Paul wanted to
leave when he did for his own private
reasons. The Jam had never stood still
and did not need any grand gestures
to cauterise the end. Despite what
anybody thought or said at the time,
without doubt, The Jam and what
we achieved, gave the three of us a
direction and changed our lives. I am
forever amazed that our music still
means so much to whoever discovers
it and I am grateful to you all._

(Twink)

(Twink)

DISCOGRAPHY 1982

ALBUM RELEASES

The Gift
Polydor. Released 12 March 1982. Chart position: 1.

Dig the New Breed
Polydor. Released 10 December 1982. Chart position: 2.

SINGLE RELEASES

Town Called Malice / Precious
Polydor. A 12" was also issued that included a live version of 'Town Called Malice'. Released 29 January 1982. Chart position: 1.

Just Who is the 5 O' Clock Hero?/ War / The Great Depression
Dutch Import. Polydor. Also issued as a 12". Released 11 June 1982. Chart position: 8.

The Bitterest Pill (I ever had to Swallow) / Pity Poor Alfie / Fever
Polydor. Released 10 September 1982. Chart position: 2.

Beat Surrender / Shopping
Polydor. Also issued as a double pack that included Beat Surrender/Shopping/Move On Up/ Stoned Out Of My Mind/War. Polydor. Released 26 November 1982. Chart position: 1.

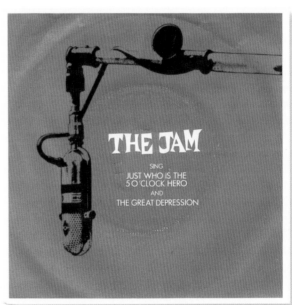

SOURCES

(Victor Watts/Rex Shutterstock)

Barney Hoskyns, 'Live review, The Jam: Fair Deal, Brixton, London', *NME*, 20 March 1982.

Barry Cain, *Flexipop* interview, 1982, *57 Varieties of Talk Soup*, Red Planet 2016.

Bryan Morrison, *Have A Cigar!*, Quiller Publishing, 2019.

Chris Catchpole, 'Paul Weller: "The Style Council Taught Me To Not Be a Cunt"', *Esquire*, 31st October 2020.

Chris Salewicz, 'The Paul Weller Interview', *The Face*, May 1982.

Dan Jennings's *Desperately Seeking Paul Weller* podcast.

Dennis Munday interview courtesy of Matteo Sedazzari.

Paul Weller promotional interview for the release of *The Gift 30th Anniversary Deluxe Edition*, UMC.

The Jam: Made In Britain, BBC Radio 6 Music documentary, 2002. Producers: Frank Wilson and Dave Barber.

Gary Crowley interview with Bruce Foxton and Rick Buckler for DVD Release *From The Jam – A First Class Return*, Invisible Hands Music, 2008.

Keith Cameron, 'Direction Reaction Creation', *NME*, May 1997.

Muriel Gray interview with Paul Weller, *The Tube*, 5 November 1982.

Paolo Hewitt, 'The Jam Meet Paolo Hewitt On Tour In Japan', *Melody Maker*, 3rd July 1982.

Paul du Noyer, 'Wham Bam Thank You Jam, The Jam, Wembley Arena', *NME*, 11 December 1982.

Paul Lester, 'Paul Weller: Last Man Standing'. *Uncut*, 1998

Paul Weller interview with Mark Cooper, 'Whine, Women and Song', *Record Mirror*, 17 July 1982.

Penny Valentine, 'Letter From Britain: Jammed Up, Jelly Tight', *Creem* , June 1982.

'Pete Townshend on The Jam', Time Out, March 12–18, 1982.

Phil Sutcliffe, 'Paul Weller: The *MOJO* Interview', *MOJO*, 2004

Richard Skinner interviews The Jam, BBC Radio 1, 27 February 1982.

Rick Buckler, 'The Ten Best Songs By The Jam', *LouderSound*, May 23, 2015.

Rick Buckler, Ian Snowball, *The Dead Straight Guide To The Jam*, Red Planet, 2017.

Simon Wells, 'The Jam: December 11th 1982', Modculture.co.uk, September 2011.

Thomas H Greene, 'Q&A: Mick Talbot of The Style Council', *The Arts Desk*, 7 Novemnber 2020.

Valerie Siebert, 'Present & Correct : The Jam's Final Album The Gift Revisited', *The Quietus*, November 2012

ACKNOWLEDGEMENTS

The authors would like to thank the following people for their involvement in, and assistance with, this book:

David Barraclough, Claire Browne, Lora Findlay and the team at Omnibus Press; Mark Brzezicki (and Neil Saint for connecting us); Barry Cain, for the kind permission to mine his 1982 *Flexipop!* interview; Gary Crowley, for the interview, for contacts, encouragement, permissions and much more besides; Mark Ellen; Mark Baxter for facilitating and liaising and Louisa, partner of the greatly missed Simon Wells, for hunting out items from Simon's archive; David at ModCulture HQ for the kind permission to use Simon Wells's feature on The Jam's final show; Sarah Hall at BBC Radio 6 Publicity; Chris Catchpole; Keith Cameron, Mark Cooper (via Charlie Viney); Phil Sutcliffe; Paul du Noyer; Paolo Hewitt; Barney Hoskyns and *Rock s Back Pages*; Dylan Howe; Gavin Martin; Jennie Matthias (and Tessa Pollitt for connecting us); Dennis Munday (and Matteo Sedazzari, for the use of his 2022 interview); Steve Nichol; Mat Osman; Eddie Piller (and Dean Chalkley for connecting us); Chris Salewicz, for the kind permission to use his 1982 Weller interview from *The Face*; Valerie Siebert at *The Quietus*; Pennie Smith; Ian Snowball; Jamie Telford; Neil 'Twink' Tinning; Simon Wells, who instigated this project; Nicky Weller (courtesy Dan Jennings / *Desperately Seeking Paul Weller* podcast); Peter Wilson. Thanks also to Den Davis for sharing his Jam collection with all those that came to The Jam exhibition 'About the Young Idea'.

(Rex Shutterstock)